I0123366

MURDER
THY
NEIGHBOR

BY
WILLIAM TERRY
RUTHERFORD

©William Terry Rutherford All Rights Reserved
ISBN-13: 9780615707082

ISBN-10: 0615707084

LCCN 2012918450

William Terry\Rutherford

Highland Park, Illinois

Contents

In The Beginning

I consider myself a peaceful man who grew up in a tough neighborhood. I was no stranger to confrontation. My wife had passed away about six years before. I did not want to live out the rest of my life without a significant other, but I had my doubts if I would ever find another woman with whom to share my life. As so often can happen, or so I have heard, I found someone as soon as I stopped looking.

It was on a summer night. I was sitting at the bar in a very nice Mexican restaurant. I ordered some food and a beer and was watching the bartender make drinks when two women walked in, one very young, around twenty-three and the other more my age. The restaurant was busy; the only two seats that were empty at the bar were the two seats next to me. The younger one sat down next to me. I struck up a conversation with the two women but do not remember what first words I blurted out. The woman more my age, in her fifties was the first to answer. She asked my last name. I told her, "Smith, Thomas Smith." She said that she remembered me from the good old days, when we were in our early twenties. I asked her name.

"Barbara Rivers."

"Rivers? Is your husband named Daniel?"

"Yes, he passed away over five years ago."

"I'm very sorry to hear that. He was a really nice guy."

"Thank you, he was a good man."

"Wow, my wife passed away not too long ago. I do not think you knew her. Beverly Stanton was her name. She was not from around here.

"No, I don't remember knowing her."

Barbara and I knew each other years before. We had hung out at the same places. She and I were not friends then, but I did remember seeing her around. I knew her husband better. Daniel and I had been casual friends. Barbara and I had a few things in common: we discovered that neither of us ever had any children and our families did not live in the state. At about that time in our conversation, when we both were talking over the girl in the middle, she received a telephone call from her boyfriend. The young girl asked Barbara if it was 'okay' to leave her at the bar.

She said, "Yes, go see him. I will be fine here. I've known Thomas for years."

Barbara lived within walking distance of the restaurant, so the young girl excused herself, leaving Barbara and me alone to talk. I was not interested in the younger woman, but I thought Barbara was quite nice looking and very interesting. I closed the gap between us at the bar, sitting in the empty chair left by Barbara's friend. I offered to buy her another beer, and she accepted. Then my food came, but I did not want to try to eat and talk. The bartender put the platter in front of me and asked me if, there was anything else I needed.

"Wow! That is a lot of food. Barbara, will you share this with me?"

She finished her beer and said, "Sure. Why not?"

I did not start to eat.

"Bartender, could we have another plate, please? We are going to share this meal. And please bring us two more beers."

I looked at her for approval for ordering another beer without first asking. It was not a problem. When the extra plate came, the bartender offered to split it for us. We both ate slowly, trying not to talk with our mouths full, so the food lasted a while. To wash down the food, we both sipped our beers. We were having a good time. I asked for two more beers, and again she did not object.

I asked if she was dating anyone at that time. She told me that for her there was no significant other in her life. Just like a woman to use the term "no significant other." Made me wonder what "other significant" there could be.

There were tables set up outside on the sidewalk to take advantage of the summer night, so I suggested we go out to them after we finished our dinner. The night was perfect – not too hot and not too cool – just a beautiful late summer night.

We talked and talked. We knew many of the same people, which made the conversation comfortably easy, and the time slipped by. We both had to work the next day, so I suggested that we continued the conversation later. I asked for her telephone number. She gave it to me with a smile. I walked her part of the way home, not knowing exactly how far would be okay. I did not want to goof this thing up.

"Are you sure you want to walk the rest of the way home? I could drive you."

"No. It is really nice out, and I like to walk."

I smiled and said, "Okay." She smiled back, and then our eyes met for just a bit longer than that of two people who had just met. I went back to my apartment feeling good about this, and it was not just the beer thinking – I really felt a connection.

I waited the customary two days before I called her, practicing how I was going to ask her out. I called asking her out, she accepted, and we made a date to go out to dinner. There was an art fair going on in the middle of town, so I knew that conversation after dinner would not be a problem. I felt it would just flow comfortably from where it left off the other night.

Barbara was renting a large house for a price that was way under the market value. She and her husband had lived there for many years. She had a seventy-pound dog and an eighteen-pound cat. She told me a wild story about how the dog found the cat.

"Daniel and I, were out sightseeing in the forest preserve with our chocolate lab. It was the middle of the week. We both had the day off, and the forest preserve was deserted. JJ listened to commands very well, so we let her off her leash to run for a while in a grassy area that was surrounded by trees. Daniel threw the ball so that she could run and fetch it. On the third throw of the ball, she caught the scent of something and ran into the woods, so far that we could not see her, and we ran after her. We used the "come" command, but JJ did not respond. She could not hear anything; she was intoxicated by the scent. We were starting to panic at the thought of losing the dog, but we just kept calling, JJ, come!"

"Finally, we saw her come out of the woods. She had something in her mouth, and as she came closer, it became slightly visible. I thought, 'Oh, I hope it is not a skunk,' as we saw the creature move. We knew it was alive. As she got closer, we realized it was a tiny tiger-striped kitten."

"She held the kitten so gently in her mouth as she walked up to us and laid it at our feet. Daniel and I were speechless. I looked for the mother cat or any people who might have claim to it. Since there was no one even looking for the kitten, we took him home with us. The next day we posted signs in and around where we found the kitten. One week, two weeks passed, and there were zero calls. So now what could we do? The kitten lay there sleeping, cuddled up to JJ. Yes, she thought the kitten was her baby. As any good mother would, she licked, protected, and cared for him. Of course, we just could not give away the kitten as it was now JJ's baby, so we decided to keep the kitten. After $160.00 in shots at the animal hospital, we added one new member to our family."

"What a great story, Barbara. Do you still have the dog and the cat?"

"Yes, JJ is twelve years old. The cat is now eight years old. He answers to Boy. We tried to name him something else but he answered to Boy, so that is his name. Boy thinks he is a dog. If you throw the practice golf ball, Boy will go retrieve it and bring it back for you to throw again. He does not know when to stop; as long as you throw it, he will go get it and bring it back. He will not quit. You have to quit first."

We dated for six months. We were happy to find someone, life is just so much better when it is shared with another. One night we agreed that life would be easier for both of us if I were to move into her house. My lease was up for renewal in two weeks. We made a rather quick decision to live together. Before moving in she warned that living in her house might be difficult because of the older couple who lived in the house next to us. I figured, how hard could this be, getting along with this older couple? I had seen them on many occasions while going to pick up Barbara for a date, and while not outwardly friendly, they looked harmless enough, so I disregarded her warning. Again she strongly stated that they could be most difficult to deal with. She stated that in the past there were periods when life would be somewhat peaceful and others when they would just get crazy. The littlest thing could set them off and make them want to go to war. I worked with difficult people all day long, so I assured her that I could handle any problems that might arise.

"I am actually anxious to apply my people skills with them."

She just looked at me and expelled a blast of air, throwing her head back with a smile.

The couple was in their seventies. She was five feet six inches tall with un-natural jet-black shoulder length hair. Barbara said that she had never seen her hair any other color. The husband stood about six feet four inches tall with white hair and a long white mustache. The hair on his upper lip waxed and twirled to a thin circle at both ends. Neither of them ever smiled. Their faces had no smile lines; they looked permanently frozen in a scowl. I attempted to be neighborly and say things like, "What nice weather we have had lately," but all I received was a mumbled "Hi." His eyes rose to meet mine and then, with a deadpan expression, he looked away, shaking his head from side to side as if to say that he was disgusted by my existence on the planet. At first I did not know what to make of this behavior. I thought that maybe there was something medically wrong with Rudy. Then I experienced a similar response from Bulla. Perhaps they were humorous people and trying to pull one over. Could this have been an ongoing joke? I asked Barbara about Bulla and Rudy's bizarre behavior.

She said, "Thomas, clearly it is no joke. This is just how they are. They have always been a little like that but as they get older they are getting worse."

"Worse how? What does that mean?"

"You would not believe it if I told you. You can be sure their neighborly rudeness will raise its ugly head in the very near future."

I know now that she was not being completely forthcoming. Perhaps she was thinking they would scare me off from moving in or by some miracle that they would change. She did, however, warn me there could be cloudy days ahead and she was right. Problems started with them all too soon after Barbara gave me her warning.

LEAF JOB

It was the end of fall. The sky had turned gray, the temperature had dropped, and leaves were falling off the trees daily. It seemed as though Rudy was always raking. Every time I pulled in the driveway, he was raking.

Barbara had a landscaping service that came on Wednesdays to cut the grass and remove the leaves. Late one Saturday, I went out to rake some leaves around the house and tidy things up. On our block all the houses faced east. Across the street were the railroad tracks for the commuter train that took people back and forth from the suburbs to the city. Our suburb had planted grass, bushes, and trees which made the tracks not visible to the houses on the west side of the street.

Barbara said, "The city has rules preventing us from raking any leaves across the street onto city land."

"I have seen Rudy rake his leaves over there. Isn't that against the city code?"

"Yes, it is against code. Rudy thinks somehow it is okay for him to do anything he wants, yet if he sees you do it he will call the police." Just do not rake the leaves over there, Thomas. If he sees you rake them over there, he will probably call the police to get you a ticket for dumping."

"That is insane, I just saw him rake his leaves over there, in front of Anna's house."

"Rudy is a little off and does not play by civilized rules."

"What about his wife?"

She is the same, just as bad, if not worse."

I went out and raked our driveway and the walkways. There were not many leaves, so the job went quick. It made our house look better for now until Wednesday when our lawn service would come to do the complete job.

I looked out the side window the next morning and found that all the work I had done was for naught. At first I thought the wind just blew all the leaves back yet

Rudy's place was immaculate. Something just was not right.

Barbara had told me that raking leaves across the street was against city code, but remember him raking the leaves across the street. I noticed that he raked them not directly across from his house but slightly in front of the house to his right or left. If the city inspectors came down this neighborhood street or if someone complained they would notice the piles of leaves on the city property. Anna might be blamed, or we might, for dumping the leaves on the city parkway in front of our houses.

I went to the front door and looked out the window. Just then, I noticed a police squad car was driving up and stopping in front of Anna's house.

"Barbara, come here quick. You have to see this. I don't know what to make of it."

Barbara came and said with an aggravated tone to her voice, "What?"

"Look at what is going on here. It looks like Anna is being blamed for something Rudy did. Is that possible?"

"Oh, yeah. That happens." Barbara said this with such an easy tone to her voice, almost as if she was asking, "What is on TV tonight?"

Rudy was outside with a rake in his hands. It seemed as though he was waiting for the police. The officer came out of his car while Rudy was pointing to the pile of leaves across the street. Just then his southern neighbor Anna came running out of her house. She started yelling and waving her arms. Rudy responded by saying something while waving his arms pointing at the pile of leaves and then Anna started to yell while pointing at the leaves. I heard her yelling out something like, "I did not rake the leaves there, he did." She was pointing to Rudy. Just then Bulla came running out of her house screaming at the top of her lungs at the officer. She started to wave her arms around like a wild woman as well. The police officer started to point at Anna's front yard. The leaves were still there. She had not raked yet.

Rudy yelled, "She did it yesterday and the day before."

I must admit Rudy was a quick-thinking liar. However, the officer was not buying it. He simply got back into his squad car and left the three of them standing there. I turned my head to say something to Barbara but when I looked back everyone was gone.

"Thomas, with Rudy, Bulla, and Anna, anything is possible. They have been going at it for years. Some years ago, Anna and her husband built up their back yard by adding dirt to it. When it rained all the water ran off her property into Rudy's back yard and vegetable garden. It caused flooding and damaged their gardens. Ever since that flooding, it has been war. They have been fighting for years and years."

Barbara went on to tell me the story. "Anna's husband passed away seven years ago. Her two boys grew up, moved out and are now living on their own, as is her daughter. The kids wanted her to move out of that house because Rudy and Bulla's attacks seemed to be coming more often and the two seemed to be taking it up a notch, but she refused to leave the house that she grew up in and raised her children in. She also refused to have Rudy and Bulla run her off her land. That is what I think they were trying to accomplish, running Anna out of her family home. Nothing will stop Bulla and Rudy. Now, with her children gone and husband passed away, she lives there alone to fight the battle. Anna is a tough one. She just does not stay completely passive. She comes back with a trick or two of her own. Seems as if nothing will stop Bulla and Rudy; they never seem to run out of stupid little annoyances to torture that poor woman. This is why I told you to be careful with them. They never let anything go. It becomes a war with them. Forgiveness is not in their vocabulary, just revenge."

"Revenge for how long? Did you say the backyard flooding thing happened over ten years ago?"

"Over twenty years. I told you they are mean, crazy people."

"Barbara, what else happened between them to cause all this bitterness?"

"A bunch of little things kept the war going but I have to say that the one big thing that seems to have started it all was the backyard flooding. You see, for Rudy and Bulla, tending their lawn and garden is their ongoing purpose in life. Anything that could upset that cart would be a major disaster. Anna is no saint in all this. She gets her licks in too. Once Rudy planted a row of bushes too close to Anna's property. Anna has a chainsaw and she proceeded to cut them in half. She was within her legal rights to do so as the plants were overhanging on her property."

"Sorry I missed that. That had to be good for a laugh."

"I guess she just couldn't take all the sniping Rudy continued to use on her."

"Did that at least slow him down?"

"Not in the least. If anything, it just made them meaner."

From all fighting they all had become experts on city neighbor codes. They used the law and the police all the time. Bulla and Rudy had some sort of "in" with the lawyers at the city's Senior Citizen's Advocate Bureau. When Anna did anything that could be against city code, Bulla and Rudy would call it in immediately. One weekend Anna's sister came to visit her. She cut the turn into Anna's driveway a little too tight and her back wheel made an impression in the mud on Bulla's side of the driveway, on their parkway. Rudy started yelling and confronted the sister while Bulla called the police on her. I had to go out to see what was going on. The officer was standing on Anna's property and getting very angry with Rudy.

He blurted out, "You get back on your driveway."

Rudy began to speak but the officer quickly cut him off in mid-sentence and this time he was much louder. In a commanding voice he said, "Get back over there," pointing his finger where he wanted Rudy to stand. Then in an angry voice he said to Rudy, "You are being ridiculous." He went back to his squad and pulled away.

Much to our amazement, in about ten minutes, two squad cars showed up. Rudy had called the police on the police!

"Wow that is beyond my ideas about neighbor wars. Why do the police keep coming when they call?"

"Because it is the law. They must investigate when anyone calls. Believe me; the police are pretty fed up with them. They cannot do anything about it. If the police did not come and something bad really happened the city and police could get sued. No matter how ridiculous or petty the call may turn out to be, the police have to answer the call and write a report. They both know this city rule and use this to aggravate one another."

When the second police car showed up, the officer simply parked in front of their driveways, got out of his car, and walked around it. Looking down as if he had lost something, he got back into his squad car and drove off without saying a word.

Observing the police action with Anna and Rudy was amusing but if the police came to our house it would not be funny.

Barbara said in a definite tone, "Oh, they will be here, probably sooner than you think."

"Why? We didn't do anything."

"We don't have to do anything; they make things up."

A few weeks would go by and things would seem peaceful. We would not see the cops or hear any arguing for weeks. Then something would happen and the fireworks would begin once again.

"How old were Anna's kids when all this started?"

"Anna grew up in that house, so the kids grew up in the house. Right now the oldest one would be around forty-five. This is part of the reason I told you to watch out for them. I have had big problems with Bulla and Rudy in the past myself. I was caught in the middle on several occasions. I do not want to start a neighbor war with either of them."

"Problems? Tell me a few problems that you had with them."

"Well, there was the time when someone threw red paint on Rudy and Bulla's white siding on their house. Anna and her children were questioned by the police; someone told the police that I threw the paint. When the police came to me I had just gotten back from vacation. I was not home at the time of the vandalizing and had the old boarding pass to prove it. Before I left for vacation I'd had some friends over. We were not loud; it was late, around midnight on a Friday. Rudy and Bulla called the police and said we were making all this loud noise. The music was not loud and these kids were not the loud type. It just bugged Bulla and Rudy when they saw us having a good time. Some of the people at the party took objection to them calling the police. As my guests left Rudy was outside in front of his house giving them dirty looks. A mini war broke out that night. Harsh words were exchanged between Rudy and my guests. I went on vacation at four that morning right after the party. When I came home from vacation I was unpacking when the police came to my house and accused me of throwing the paint."

"Who accused you of throwing the paint, Rudy or Anna?"

"The police would not say. Bulla, Rudy, or Anna's children. Who knows? It doesn't matter now. A few months later Bulla and Rudy received a card, in the mail for New Year's that wished them 'no more new years.' Now, because of the party, Bulla was angry with me and so she accused me of sending the card. She called the police. I was in Denver during the time the post mark was on the card; it was also mailed from a suburb where one of Ann's sons lived."

"Oh my! That was not nice of Anna again. If you made me guess, I'm thinking it was Anna's boys that did the paint and the card. Thank God you were out of town on both occasions."

"Yep, nothing is worse than being accused of something when you're completely innocent. After the paint job Rudy put up lights in his driveway. Anna and Rudy's driveways run next to each other. When he turns them on, the lights are so strong covering every inch of that driveway. They actually light up both houses. You could place a chair in any part of either driveway and read a book. I never saw lights so bright in a residential area."

"Well, I'm beginning to see what you mean about Rudy and Bulla. These two could actually become dangerous. However, I let my apartment go, and I love you, so I am not going anywhere. Looks as though I will have to deal with whatever comes up."

"Just don't end up in jail."

SNOW JOB

There was one nice thing about the weather changing from fall to winter and the shorter colder days: this meant that I would not have to see Rudy outside every day. I felt relief in not having to pull into our driveway with those incriminating eyes just staring at us all the time. When they were not outside and in their house, I could not help think that they were looking, peeking out from behind their closed blinds. The feeling of being watched all day and night really wore on our minds.

One Saturday morning in mid-December, the first snow of the winter fell. Over three inches were down and mounting. Once the depth went over three inches, we would have to shovel the un-paved driveway or we would not be able to get the cars in or out. The snow was going to stick; the temperature was dropping, the drive-way would require shoveling. Late Saturday, when it stopped snowing, I grabbed the shovel to clear the drive-way so that we could pull our cars in and out on Sunday. I grabbed the shovel and as I passed Barbara, she looked at me suspiciously.

"What are you going to shovel?"

"The snow in the damn driveway, so that we can pull out our cars tomorrow morning without them getting stuck."

"Okay. But do not shovel any snow on Bulla's and Rudy property."

"Where does their property start?"

"They think it starts where they put that white brick wall up on their side of our driveway."

"Do you mean that six-inch-high row of white stone?"

"Yes."

I remember the white bricks from the summer. Now the bricks had been covered with snow. I really did not understand. When I had shoveled a driveway or side-walk, I had always put the snow on either side of the driveway or walk. Who cared as long as it was out of the way and not on a walkway? It was just snow and would melt soon.

The driveway would fit one car in the entrance. Halfway down the driveway, it widened out to fit two cars side by side. The snow was rather fluffy and in general it was about four or five inches deep. I got tired of shoveling the snow from the left side of our driveway to the right side, so I dumped a small amount of our snow on their property. I did it in a stealthy manner so as not to make it obvious. I put less than ten shovels of snow on their side.

It was getting dark and I was cold and tired. I retreated to the warm house to watch some sports on television while having a beer or two. It was good to be in the house staying warm. The snow had stopped; the weatherman said that no further snow should fall that evening.

The next day I threw on a coat and went out to the cars to make sure it had not snowed more the previous night. Stepping out on the porch I looked at the driveway and was befuddled; it just looked wrong. Upon closer inspection, I found heaps of snow in the driveway. At first I just did not understand. It had not snowed, when I checked the sidewalks and the street they had no extra snow on them, yet our driveway was full of snow. Even more snow than there was the previous day. What had caused this? Upon closer examination, I saw the snow was not even. Someone had purposely heaped it in mounds. For a moment I wondered if I had shoveled yesterday or had I dreamed that I had shoveled yesterday. Either that or I did a real bad job shoveling the previous day. I hastened my way back into the house to retrieve the snow shovel.

"Barbara, am I losing my mind, or did I not shovel the driveway yesterday?"

"Yes, you did. Do you have a problem?"

"Yeah, there are mounds of snow in the driveway and it did not snow since I shoveled yesterday."

"Did you shovel some snow on their property from our driveway?"

"Maybe a couple of shovels, so little that I thought it would not be noticeable."

"Well, Rudy notices every flake. He probably came out to inspect your snow removal job. When he noticed that you shoveled some snow his way he decided to give it back to you. He might have been watching you through his blinds when you were shoveling. I asked you not to shovel any snow on his property."

"That is ridiculous. He did not just shovel what I put on his side. You could hardly notice what I put on his side. He shoveled all the snow he could find back into our driveway. Is he insane? Our cars are unable to pull out because he shoveled so much snow into our driveway."

"Yes. Next time when you shovel the driveway do not put any on his side."

I had to sit down. My face felt hot, my jaw clenched, and the hair on the back of my neck began to rise. I had never encountered anyone so unreasonable. This was just plain crazy and mean. Barbara had warned me not to shovel any snow over there. It was a small amount of snow that I threw on his side, his reaction to that small amount of snow was to dump fifty times the amount of snow I shoveled on his side. Seeing all that snow in our driveway was infuriating. As I looked at the amount of snow he put there, I noticed that he had to get snow from the other side of his house to get enough to mound up and block our cars in our driveway. Why would he do such a thing? It seemed like a lot of work for nothing. I was beginning to see what Barbara meant when she warned me that Rudy and Bulla could be a problem.

I counted to ten but that did not work, so I counted to one hundred, waiting for my blood pressure to return to some level of normality. I was really trying to suppress the anger for the sake of keeping the peace for Barbara. I went back out and cleared our driveway cursing to myself the whole time.

I gave it a few days without saying anything. When I came home on Thursday, I observed Rudy on his front walkway with a broom dusting off his sidewalk.

"Rudy, may I have a minute of your time?"

I walked toward him. He stood in the middle of his walkway and took no steps forward to meet me. He just turned to face me, holding his broom like a rifle diagonally in front of him. He stared at me as I approached him.

"Listen Rudy, if I offended you by shoveling snow on your property, I'm sorry. I did not know you would take such offense to it. I only put a few shovels of snow over there."

His answer was, "Huh."

"You, however, shoveled a huge amount of snow into our driveway. Next time something of this nature occurs that angers you, please do not over-react. Just talk to me."

"I don't know what you're talking about. Don't threaten me." His voice became increasingly louder. "Don't threaten me. You're threatening me!"

A neighbor was coming down the sidewalk towards us. I was facing Rudy, so I could not see the neighbor approaching. Rudy used this opportunity to attempt to incriminate me.

Rudy barked out, "Don't threaten me. I will call the police." He then turned to the neighbor and said, "You heard him. He threatened my life. You're my witness."

I said, "Oh, no! Hey, I didn't threaten him."

I looked at the neighbor passing by, trying to read his face, to see if he believed this crazy person making these accusations. I felt I had to defend myself for something I did not do.

"I didn't threaten him. He was shoveling snow onto my driveway."

Rudy just stood there motionless, just standing there with his broom staring at the passing neighbor.

"No, no, no." I said as I began to stumble with my explanation. I was afraid I might look guilty to the neighbor walking by, the more I tried to explain, the worse I sounded.

The snow thing that I was trying to discuss with Rudy was now lost in these false accusations. I saw the neighbor turn his head and walk straight away from us. He wanted no part of this disagreement. When the neighbor walked away I looked at Rudy and thought to myself, 'no sense in reasoning with this whack job.' Rudy was smirking; he looked as if he just had eaten a nice meal. He was proud of his little performance. I made a resolution never try to reason with this mad man again. I turned and just walked away; no talking to this person.

Barbara and I were sitting in the kitchen having a glass of wine after dinner. She had picked up a couple of bottles of chardonnay white wine while she was visiting her sister in California. It somehow tasted better knowing that she bought it right from the grower. The wine just had that down-to-earth quality that was making us feel quite relaxed and happy. I had dealt with Rudy and Bulla for several months, and Barbara was relieved that I had not gone running off after taking my fair share of abuse from those two.

Our conversation turned from them to us. She mentioned that she had a great health plan at work that included dental. We had become partners in every way; we both brought home the same amounts in salary. By sharing the expenses we had been paying the monthly bills much more easily. She thought it would be advantageous if we got married. I quickly answered with a yes. I suggested not making a big deal out of it and she agreed. I suggested getting it done in December, before January first, for income tax purposes.

She said that she would call the courthouse the next day and check on when we could get the license and get married. She came back with the date of December 23, a Saturday. A Judge would marry us right after he set bond for the Friday night drunks. To get the license we had to show our birth certificates and two other forms of identification. We bought the license on Thursday for our Saturday wedding and we both would have to sign the document in front of an officer of the court on Saturday just before we could see the Judge.

I knew that we were doing the right thing. We were both very happy to be married again, as we had been for most of our adult lives. We just had so much in common and we understood each other.

Our appointment with the Judge and our destiny was for nine o'clock. The clerk suggested we show up ten minutes early but we were the type of people who would always be five to twenty-five minutes early. There were seven couples waiting to get married that day. We had really thought that we would be the only ones. We all picked numbers out of a hat to see who went first; we picked number three. The Judge was reading the vows off a plastic card and from what I could hear from where we were sitting, he was reading fast. One was gone, then two, and then number three was called to come forward. We raised our hands as if we were stretching for the clouds. It kind of felt like school; he had such a quick pace going we did not want to miss our turn. I had a sports watch with a timer on it, so when the Judge spoke his first words of our marriage vows, I started the stopwatch. I stopped it on "I now pronounce you man and wife." The total time was two minutes fifty-seven seconds with a cost of twenty-seven dollars. My birthday was December 27. I would have thought that my lucky number could be 27, if I were superstitious. Time would tell how lucky it would be.

IN THE SPRING,
IN THE DRIVEWAY

Winter turned to spring and the clean warm air just felt good. I drove home from work with the windows lowered to feel the fresh warm air. There in our driveway stood Rudy, this six-foot four figure, working on his plants. He was halfway up the driveway. I pulled my car up to within ten feet of him but he did not move from my path. It was as if he was daring me to run him over. He had heard the car pull in but just stood erect and looked in my direction. He did not budge. He stared with an expression-less face, bent back over, and went back to grooming his flowers, plants, and shrubs. He was not going to move, so I just drove the car around him.

Barbara was coming home later and she needed room to park in the driveway. Most days we left work at different times. She had exact working hours; I never knew when I would get done with my work. The next day I left work early and sure enough, there was Rudy, working on his plants from our driveway. He was not moving. I honked my horn. He stood up, looked at me, and then went back to doing whatever he was doing. One minute, two, three going on four, I could not understand what this person was trying to prove. I drove around him again, opened the car door, got out, and passed the evil one with the white hair and mustache. I know I had said before that I could not reason with this guy after he accused me of threatening him but he was impossible to avoid, he being right there and having impeded the advancement of my car. I said hello just to see how he would handle a greeting. He did not look up, nor did he respond immediately. Then, in a low guttural tone, a sound came. I could not make out what he was trying to say. I walked around him and went into the house to wait for Barbara. I could ask her to explain this unorthodox behavior from him. I suppressed my annoyance and just sat on the couch, thinking. Now I was the one shaking my head, remembering the conversation with Barbara where she said, "You will see! Ha!"

I had never encountered an individual with this demeanor. It presented a dilemma in that I just did not know how to combat such an individual. Was he was still ticked off, about the driveway snow incident that occurred way back in the winter.

Barbara came home thirty minutes later.

"Hi honey. How was your day?" I asked her.

"I'm so tired. Work was hell today."

I felt for her. I put off telling her about my driveway issue until the end of dinner when she opened the door to the conversation for me.

"What time did you get home from work?"

"About thirty minutes before you. I have to ask you something. Does Rudy usually work on his garden from our driveway?

"Yes."

"When you pull in does he move out of our driveway to let you park?"

"No."

"Oh well, then I will have a talk with him."

Barbara's face changed like someone just told her a bad joke..

"No, don't start anything. You said last winter that you could not reason with them. He probably still carry-ing a grudge about the show you shoved on his side. We have had peace with them the last several months, and I do not want them to start them up again."

"That was winter. He was not outside much. From what I can remember from last summer and fall, he was outside all day long. You want me to settle down and not to start anything. What gives him the right? I am not going to take this intimidation. I refuse to be bullied."

"Thomas, just let this go and do not start anything with them. I have been living here a long time. I warned you I could not explain this kind of behavior before because I knew you would not believe me. Now you see what I have been dealing with for all these years. Can you please just let it go?"

I did not want to make Barbara uncomfortable. I should not have let it go but I did. I walked away scratching my head. I was really pondering Barbara's forbidding warning.

I couldn't understand this type of behavior because I had never dealt with any human beings who acted toward their fellow men with such contempt and bitterness that seemingly came from nowhere.

As I had discovered several months after moving into my new residence, Rudy was always outside, working on the bushes, lawn, flowers, or grass, or just sweeping the cement. As for Bulla, she too was out quite often, just not as much as Rudy. It seemed he was outside all the daylight hours.

They were both retired and obsessive about their lawn and flowers. I would come home from work at a different time each day. Rudy was outside nine out of ten days. He was usually in our driveway kneeling down working on his plants and shrubs. I would pull in the driveway and stop, leaving around fifteen feet between my car and him. When he heard me drive in he would look around to make sure my car had stopped, then without moving out of the way continue his gardening. He made me drive around him to park. I would try to make nice by saying hello or trying some small talk like, "Good weather for a change." There was never any response; just a mumble of something in such a low voice that I could not make out what he was saying.

I kept saying to myself, "Keep the peace, he will get tired of this child like behavior."

I knew better than to keep repressing these annoyances. My anger would just simmer until one day it would just explode. I was kidding myself thinking that I might get used to it or maybe they might all of a sudden turn into nice neighbors. I said nothing, trying to ignore it.

Five weeks had passed and he still was in our driveway, preventing me from driving straight in. When Barbara came home from work, I began telling her of my uncomfortable encounter.

"They are crazy. Just ignore them. We are better off saying nothing. Just drive around him," was her emphatic reply.

"Okay, this is not working for me." I reluctantly replied.

Barbara worked very hard at her job. Sunday came and I suggested we start the gas grill in the back yard for some brats or hamburgers for dinner. We had a small cement patio where a garage once stood. Our outdoor furniture consisted of an old iron table, four chairs, and a gas grill. Rudy and Bulla had a cement open-air patio with a sun umbrella, table, and four chairs, and a six-foot privacy fence so that even though we were within earshot of what they said, we could not see each other.

Barbara and I gathered everything we needed to have our outdoor dinner and lit the grill. As we were just sitting there waiting for the grill to get hot we heard Bulla and Rudy come out and pop some cans of something to drink. It sounded as if they had rehearsed their conversation prior to coming outside.

Bulla started, "Rudy, this new guy is really bad news."

Rudy chimed in, "You're right. Barbara's first husband was a much nicer person. Where do you think she found this guy?"

Bulla stated, "I have no idea. Probably some trailer park somewhere. He is just trailer trash."

We could hear them as plain as day. I was in shock. What does one say to such a statement? Barbara just stared at me and I stared back into her eyes. They knew we were there because we were talking before they started and if we could hear them they certainly could hear us. They were playing this little game of insults deliberately for us to hear. I felt that I just had to say something.

Barbara came first with, "I happen to know some very nice people who live in trailers."

I shouted at them, "You know, we can hear you."

Bulla blurted out, "We are not talking to you. Mind your own business."

It was hard to believe what just had come out of Bulla's mouth. I was glad that Barbara heard the same thing to give credibility to this insanity. Then they started to talk casually about some other unfamiliar subjects as if nothing had happened. I was in shock and Barbara did not want any trouble. We went about eating our dinner. As soon as we finished eating, we cleaned up and went inside the house.

"Oh my God, do you believe what they just did?"

"I believe it but I must admit it was a shocker. Funny part is they said that they liked my late husband Daniel and that he was such a nice guy. When he was alive they hated him. Some years ago Daniel tried to help Rudy repair his fence and stepped on some vegetables in their garden in the process. They went crazy and were mad at him from that time on."

"What is wrong with those two?"

"They live in a dark place. You know their own children won't even talk to them."

"How many do they have?"

"Three."

"Come to think of it, I have never seen any cars in their driveway."

"Their kids live within ten miles of them but they never come over. I was told that they do not call on the telephone either. It's just Bulla and Rudy together, hating the world."

"It is sad but it is hard to feel sorry for them because they are just so damn mean."

Rudy usually took meticulous care of the front lawn but one day while pulling into the driveway, I noticed that his grass was turning brown in spots and dying. He was on all fours digging up the grass. I had to ask, so I stopped the car and got out.

"What's wrong, Rudy?"

"What the hell do you think I am doing?"

"I didn't ask you what you were doing. I asked you what was wrong."

"I'm getting rid of these damn grubs."

"Good luck with that. It looks like you are trying to dig them out."

Rudy snorted and began to dig into the lawn much harder than before, throwing dirt around like a kid in order to vent his anger. Barbara said they got grubs all the time in the spring but only in the front yard. Bulla would not let him use chemicals because she was afraid it would hurt her flowers.

About three weeks later, all the grass in our backyard started to turn brown. I dug down a little and sure enough, we had grubs. Barbara said we had never had grubs before, so Rudy must have taken some from his front yard and planted them in our backyard. Grubs do not fly and it was quite suspicious how they got in our backyard when we never had them before.

I bought some grub-killer in a twenty-pound bag and took it to the backyard where the grubs were eating the roots of our grass. I put on a pair of gloves, cut open the bag and began to sprinkle the granular grub killer on the infected spots.

I did not hear her come out of her house because my back was turned but all of a sudden Bulla was standing on her property line as close to our backyard as possible without standing on our lot.

"Hey, you, Tom ass or whatever your name is! Don't you get that poison anywhere near us."

Turning around to face Bulla I saw she was in a red-and-white floral housecoat that was tied at the waist. She wore backless dingy brown slippers, her coal black hair was in rollers, and she had a look of anger on her face that could stop a truck. I did not say anything. I was thinking about how she had pronounced my name, "Tom-ass." I put my hand in the bag of grub killer, pulled out a handful of granules and threw it in front of me, not even close to her property line but in her direction.

She replied "Son of a bitch," turned around and headed back into her house, probably to have a little hate session with Rudy. I am sure she exaggerated me throwing the grub-killer. She surely would tell Rudy that I threw it at her, which of course I did not. The suspicion was confirmed when Rudy came out to see if he could find any granules in their backyard. He used his foot to separate the grass where she had been standing. I thought, "What a freak show this has become."

There had to be mold or something toxic in that house that was causing this irrational behavior in them. I started to watch my back. Knowing that at any time our neighbors could go off the deep end was not a comfortable way to live.

The law will not take anyone's word for it. The law needs proof which is a good thing because if the law believed anything without evidence, even a little of what Bulla and Rudy made up and then reported it to the police, that would be enough to put Barbara and me in jail.

Yes, Rudy did call the police. The squad car pulled up in front of their house; the officer went in their front door and then Rudy and the officer came out of the back door of the house, walked to propped spot on the grass, separating it to try to find the magic poison granules. Next we had a visitor. I did not recognize this officer. He explained their complaint that I was throwing some sort of granular weed poison on their property. I denied it.

The officer said, "Very well then, I did not see anything there."

"Officer, you do know that those two are a little eccentric with their paranoid constantly complaining to the police for things that are just false."

"Mr. Smith, I assure you that everyone on the force knows who they are. I haven't seen you before. Did you just move in?"

"About a year ago."

"My condolences. Good luck sir."

I had to ask the officer, "Why don't you arrest then for making a false police report?"

The office said, "They must sign a complaint and I've never heard of them signing any complaint. If they did and it was a false report then we could arrest them. As long as they keep calling, we must follow up on the complaint and keep coming out to investigate. They know better than to sign a complaint report that has no facts to substantiate it." The officer half smiled and left the house.

OH! NOT THEIR TRUMPET VINE

The landscaping around the house needed some work, so I took it upon myself to clean up the foliage and do some weeding all around the house. There was a small tree on our property that had a six-foot vine growing on it. It looked like a weed, so I decided to rid the tree of the vine. I made a pile of the cut weeds and then noticed a very pretty flower on top of the weed pile that I had not noticed when I was weeding, yet there it was connected to that damn vine.

I stared at it and said to myself, "Oh dear. That does not look like any weed I have ever seen. It is connected, and therefore part of the vine I just cut down."

I stood back after working on the yard to observe how much nicer the backyard looked. Proud of myself except for that vine, I went in the house to wait for Barbara. It was 4:10 pm and I knew she would be home at 4:15 as usual. My palms began to sweat and it felt very warm in the house.

She showed up right at 4:15. She came in the house and I cheerfully said, "Barbara, wait till I show you what I did in the backyard."

She stopped, turned around to face me and gave me a look. I had seen that look before; it was the face she made when we were talking about Rudy and Bulla. She perceived something was wrong, very wrong. I asked myself, "How could she know that I cut the trumpet?"

"Thomas, what did you do back there?"

"I did some weed-pulling."

"Where?" she asked.

"In our backyard where that grubby tree is growing."

"Oh-no," she cried.

"What?" I said.

She went running out the back door and I followed. When she caught sight of the tree she started to shout, "No! No! You didn't."

"Didn't what?"

"You cut down her trumpet vine, the one she had been growing for five years. This year it finally flowered. It came from a hundred-year-old stock of such vines. She had been waiting, watering, and using expensive fertilization for five years. It finally bloomed this year and you cut it down."

"Well, it started on their lot but the vine grew on our lot, on our tree. I thought it was a weed and I had every legal right to cut it because it was on our property." From what little I knew of city law, I knew that was true.

"That does not matter to them. You have no idea what you just have done. They are just going to go nuts. They are going to think you did this on purpose. You get over there and apologize and I will try to find another one to buy for her."

"Oh! This could get uncomfortable."

I went over and knocked on their door. Bulla answered. She had a housecoat wrapped tightly around her with that coal black hair plastered to her head. There was no smile, just that cutting of the eye look.

With a frozen, mean, impatient look on her face she replied, "What do you want?"

"Well, Bulla, I was pulling weeds in my back-yard and Barbara said that I made a mistake and cut down a vine."

She interrupted my speech with a shriek in her voice. "The trumpet vine. You cut down my trumpet vine."

"I'm afraid so. I am very--------"

I was interrupted before I could finish my sentence with, "Wait till Rudy hears about this, you idiot."

Before I could apologize, she slammed the door in my face. I could hear her ranting behind the closed door. I could not make out specific words; it sounded like a lot of profanity. I had expected a wild reaction. The fact that it was somewhat muted made me worry much more as to what retaliation would be coming.

I looked for Barbara outside but she was not there. She was inside sitting on the couch just staring out into space. She looked sick at heart.

"What happened over there?"

"It did not go so well. She slammed the door in my face while saying, 'Rudy will get you for this.'

Her shoulders sunk and her head dropped as if it weighed too much for her to hold up any longer. It was as if she had lost it all.

"I tried to apologize, but she would have none of it. What else could I do? People make mistakes."

"What little chance we had for peace is gone. They just do not forgive. I will try to replace her vine. I don't know what good it will do. I just do not know what else to do."

"Hey, you're talking as if we are the bad guys. I did not do that on purpose."

"You don't know them the way I do. In their minds, you did it on purpose and they will try to get even. It looks like war; maybe even the forever kind like the one they have with Anna."

I just did not understand how these people thought or how they would react to someone making a mistake, trying to apologize, and offering to make amends. I was worried; it concerned me that Barbara seemed frightened by the situation. I was angry that Bulla would not let me apologize. They just assumed that I was as evil and mean as them. If I intentionally cut it down, I would not admit to cutting it down. To normal rational people that could make sense. Then it dawned on me that not all the rules applied here. Not with these two. There was nothing more I could do. I apologized and Barbara said she would find her a new plant. We just had to let it ride and see what happened.

STRANGE EVENTS

One month had passed and there had been no visible retaliation for the trumpet vine. We knew something was coming in accordance with their prior behavior.

It had not rained for over ten days. Our flowers needed a drink.

"Barbara, do we have any good metal nozzles for the hose?"

"I had a couple of brass ones but they disappeared. Probably some kids stole them."

"No problem. I will go pick us up a new one."

I bought a good brass nozzle and she said that the one I bought looked just like the one she had.

"You had better disconnect it from the hose and bring it inside or it will be gone."

"No, it couldn't happen again. It had to be a onetime thing."

In five days it was gone. Then from time to time something left outside would disappear. I was kind of a repair person and could fix many things around the house. Barbara did not have many tools; I had a bunch and brought them with me. Some of the tools I stored in the back shed. It had no door on it but it could not be seen from the driveway, so I thought it was safe. Nothing much was in there worth stealing, just some old tools, a pitchfork, hoe, pliers, old paint, a couple of jars of screws, and other odds and ends. This missing tool thing made me suspicious.

I asked Barbara to think about what other gardening tools went missing over the years.

"Two sprinklers with timers, one pitchfork, an older hoe, two metal hose nozzles, three or four special rakes, and some other odds and ends have disappeared." She stated that I should not leave anything out or someone would probably take it.

The recent events caused her to begin reflection on the past. I joked with her saying "Maybe the shed is haunted."

She did not find humor in that. It caused her to look off in space and think. Then it came to her, thinking about the shed, and she remembered something that happened before I moved in.

Barbara remembered. "After Daniel died, one day when I was cutting the grass, Bulla had complained about weeds in the driveway. I took the gas-powered mower and went over the driveway. The driveway was not paved, so some rocks were being disturbed. After two passes of the driveway, Bulla came running out of the house screaming at me. 'You are going to kill us. A rock came from that lawnmower and hit our window. If it had broken the window we could have been killed.' I had to shut off the gas mower to hear her.

"Bulla reiterated her complaint: 'A damn rock came out of that mower and hit our window. If it would have broken the glass, you could have killed me.'

Barbara said, "I almost started to laugh. Instead I restarted the mower so that I did not have to listen to that maniac rant. The sound of the mower drowned out Bulla, so I went on with the mowing and Bulla went back in the house. I couldn't afford a landscaper at that time, so I cut the grass once a week myself. The lawnmower died after the rock incident. It did not last one full season before it would not start. I kept pulling and pulling that thing to get it started. Rudy was watching me and just started laughing at me."

"Laughing at you? That guy is really not very nice. I think the normal thing for any man to do would be to try to help a neighbor, not laugh at you for not being able to start the mower."

"He just looked at me trying over and over to pull the starter. It just would not start and he laughed harder at all the effort I was putting in to get it started. His laughter seemed a bit cruel as it went on for a while. Then without saying a word he turned and walked into his house."

"They must have been angry about the stone hitting the window. I want to know more of the strange things that occurred during the years you lived here before I moved in."

Barbara explained that after the lawnmower would not start, she figured it was just a cheap one that was not any good and gave it away. It was the end of the summer and she decided that she would just deal with the grass the next year.

The next year she bought a new lawnmower, a better one this time. Halfway through the summer the new one too would not start. Not knowing what to do she just put it in the shed and let the grass grow. A few days later a new neighbor from down the street asked to borrow her lawnmower. She agreed but said that she could not get it to turn over. She told him it was practically new and she didn't know what the problem was. He said he was good with engines and would get it running for her.

Barbara was going to the store and it just so happened that she was passing his house when he was trying to start the mower. She stopped the car to see if it would start for him. On the third pull it made a loud banging sound and a cloud of black smoke rose from the mower. Her neighbor jumped back, thinking there could be a secondary explosion. Barbara got out of the car and asked him if he had been hurt. He said that he was not injured by the mower explosion but he figured he must have done something that made it all go so very wrong, so he offered to pay for the mower. Barbara, being the overly nice person she is, just told him not to worry about it. She did not think it was his fault but she really could not figure out what happened to it. She had had it with gas-powered lawnmowers, so she got out the yellow pages and hired landscapers to cut the lawn once a week.

"Didn't it dawn on you that Rudy might have had something to do with both of them not starting and the last one blowing up?"

"Not then, but now that you mention it, sabotage is a distinct possibility. At the time the lawnmowers quit working, it never occurred to me that anyone would do such a malicious and dangerous thing. I just do not think about evil people and what they are capable of doing. I used to have a hard time believing anyone would do something so horrible but now I am seeing it in a different light. Now, that makes him dangerous."

"Why in the world did you not tell me this before?"

"You never asked me, and besides, I did not consider the possibility of sabotage."

OKAY, THEN
DON'T MOVE

Rudy had a sixteen by sixteen foot steel shed in his backyard. It had an extra big lock on a single door and no windows to look in. We had a little shed that did not have a door on it. Most of our neighbors had newer garden tools than we did and I did not see the need for a secure shed.

I would not keep any costly thing in there. From then on I would have to put my tools back in the house. It was a hassle but necessary if we did not want to have our tools keep disappearing.

I think I knew where the missing tools were, but not being able to prove the items stolen were ours, we could not take any legal action on our neighbors with the large locked shed.

Several times a week, sometimes twice in a single day, Rudy would be in our driveway, bent over, working on his bushes and plants. I began to think he was there for the sole purpose of preventing me from pulling my car directly into the driveway. I just kept driving around him, wondering how long I was going to give him the right of way without confronting him.

Coming home from work after an especially hard day of putting up with customers with outrageous demands and frivolous complaints put me in a bad mood. I was certainty not in the mood for any of Rudy's nonsense. As my car approached our house I looked in the driveway. He was there, bent over in the driveway, and this time he had himself positioned more in the front of the driveway where it was narrower, only wide enough for one car.

As I looked in the driveway and noticed him bent over, I experienced a flash of anger. Instead of slowing down to pull in the driveway, I actually increased my speed. He heard the increase in the revolutions of the motor signaling the car was speeding up. I had one foot on the brake and the other on the gas. I certainly did not want to actually run him over. I just wanted to put as much of a scare into him as possible, while still not being charged with vehicular manslaughter. He stood erect and tried to jump up on his one-foot-high wall to avoid being run over. His knees were stiff from being bent, making it a very ungraceful jerky leap. Rudy could not know for sure if I had seen him in the driveway. He was jumping to save his life.

Once he had made his jump to safety I slowed my automobile as if nothing had happened. He may have figured then I never intended to run him over but he could not be 100 per cent sure of that. He could not take the chance that I would not stop the car. The thought of that tickled inside.

As I exited my auto he stood there just staring at me with contempt. I actually started to laugh. With a smile I said, "Got to be careful, almost got you that time."

The muscles in his face tightened. His shoulders followed, moving up ever so slightly. I could feel his eyes on me while I entered my house. My smile seemed to be stuck on my face as my mind's eye took a picture of his frustration. My spirit needed that to serve as a release for my ever growing, pent up frustration.

I played out the scene for Barbara. To give her an upfront visual I re-enacted the leap he made to avoid the rush of the oncoming car. She could not help but laugh.

"Tomorrow do you think Rudy will risk being in the driveway?"

"Thomas, you probably just stuck a big stick into the hornets' nest."

The next day as I turned for home at a regular pace I came upon the driveway. There was no one in my way. That silly mustache was nowhere in sight. It was just a moment of triumph that felt good. I was in the right. He was the intruder.

Days went by and I did not see him in the driveway. However, his garden looked as if it was attended to, which meant he was now timing his driveway work for when he was sure I would not be pulling in.

OUR TRUMPET VINE IS MISSING

Saturday came on a beautiful summer day. We had breakfast, fed the pets, I opened the windows and sat on the porch to just rest and take it all in. Barbara went off to the back yard to tend to her flowers. She returned shortly. "Thomas, our trumpet vine is missing.

"A plant just doesn't go missing."

"Well, go back and take a look. It is not there." Her voice sounded as if she would cry.

"Let's go look."

We walked back to the place where she had planted the two trumpet vines she bought, one for Bulla and Rudy and one for us as a gesture of friendship. Barbara knew exactly where theirs and ours were planted; their plant was intact and growing while our plant seemed to be missing. I got close to the ground and saw that the plant was cut off just before the first leaf. All that was left was a stem three inches long with no leaves, just a naked vine sticking out of the ground.

"The plant was cut off right before the first leaf."

"You are right. She cut ours off to get even with you."

"We said we were sorry. We even bought a replacement plant. Is this how civilized people act?"

"Civilized? Bulla and Rudy are not civilized. They are bad, mean, crazy people. Do you have it now?"

Barbara's sadness turned to anger and she turned and walked into the house. I waited a minute, just staring at the crime scene, trying to make sense out of this cruel act. Then I went in after Barbara.

She had found a mechanism to deal with her neighbors' constant insanity. She would just grab a book, lie on the couch with a cup of tea, and start to read. I went to the porch to sit to contemplate what, if any, action needed to be taken.

We did the Saturday shopping, came home, put away the groceries, and started on the household chores. We did not discuss the event that had no explanation except for some sort of bizarre cruelty toward someone who tried to make up for a human error. I was angered at Bulla for hurting Barbara's feelings. She had nothing to do with the vine cutting but she was paying the price for my cutting theirs down.

Barbara did try to excuse the cutting by saying, "Perhaps a rabbit could have eaten the plant."

"Ate just one trumpet vine and nothing else?"

In a sad, disheartened voice she said, "Yes, you're right. It was them."

The next day I was fussing with something in our shed and noticed Bulla walking in her backyard close to the vine. I walked over to where she was standing which was very near the trumpet vines.

"Hello Bulla. Look at this. Some rabbit must have eaten our Trumpet vine but it missed yours. How lucky for you!"

Bulla said, "I have not seen any rabbits all summer. We do not have rabbits around here."

"Well, it looks like some kind of rodent cut the vine. If not a rabbit, then one ugly rat must have eaten it."

That got her. She spun around and quickly walked out of the yard. A smile returned to my face like the smile I wore on the day when I pulled into the driveway a little too fast. I went back inside the house and began to tell Barbara what I had just done. I knew that she was going to have a negative reaction to my comment about some rodent, so I softened the event by telling her something about a rabbit eating the plants and let it go at that. Barbara wanted peace.

I did not understand how she could just keep blowing all this stuff off. When I asked her that question, her reply was that she had lived there for such a long time and there were times when she, Rudy, and Bulla all got along. I guess she was just hoping those times would return.

I refused to be bullied. When I was in high school, I was only five feet tall as a freshman. I finally started to grow in my senior year of high school; I made it up to five feet five inches tall and I would eventually end up six feet tall. I knew how mean people operated and how cruel they could be. To give in to any bully was a sentence for more of the same, first verbal moving on sometimes to physical. The mental could actually be more damaging than the physical. I was not physically strong, so I'd had to use my creativity to survive with my self-worth intact.

My father was only five foot two and I watched his social skills that he had developed over time and used to keep the bad people at bay. One defense was humor. Humor was a great deflector when one of the bad people commented on a physical defect I had. The bully would wait for around four or five other people to be around and then would come out with an insult to try to get a laugh and gain popularity with the people. I would not show hurt or anger. Those emotions are fuel for their vicious behavior. If, for example, he commented on my nose being large I would come back with, "Well, you know what they say: a large nose means he's very well endowed inside his pants" This statement was ridiculous but it had the element of humor. The group laughed even louder, looking at the bully for a retort, but he was shocked at the comeback and could not think of anything to say. Now instead of them laughing at me, their attention was diverted back to the bully. The mean bully would be speechless and actually look like a fool for making such a lame observation. He would think twice before he would try to attack verbally again.

Then, getting him alone, I would befriend him. At that point we had mutual respect and life at school could go on. I saw my father do this many times with men he worked with. I would go with him to social events sometimes and the men would sometimes drink and want to pick on the little person. He used these same skills. By the time, I was a senior I was actually well known in my class. Everyone knew my name and I really did not know many of their names, which was embarrassing. I just could not remember everyone's name. I graduated from high school at five foot five inches tall and then really started to grow. Rudy and Bulla were bullies all right, but just not the kind of bullies I had ever come across before.

High School, was a jungle indeed. At that time there was one teacher for forty or more students. Many places in school unsupervised, to get gang attacked. The boys wash room, the back lockers rarely saw a teacher go that way. The students knew the layout of every inch of the school, where and when the teachers would come down the hall. Today is the geeks back then it was the nerds, or perhaps just someone, who did not have many friends and was quiet not "fitting in". A perfect victim for usually someone physically stronger and having a few friends that hung together and I guess, out of boredom found it entertaining to pick on someone. Always being an observer of human behaviour. I discovered that at lunch, the big guy would have two or three friends around him and all three were bored. Now here comes Jonny minding his own business and for some physical or personality, difference like being shy would draw attention from this group. The big guy usually started thing first. He would test Jonny as he walked by. The big guy and his friends would say something negative, with humour put behind a hurtful phrase. If Johnny did not laugh and go along with the (joke) on him, it was for sure the start of trouble. High school and lower grads spend an enormous amount time of the day together. In the sight of supervisors, everyone behaves perfectly. It is all part of the game that has been going on for as long as people, had to spend most of their days together. Many at this age do not want to get involved. Parents just say mind your own business, don't get involved. Not wanting to be Jonny and get on the wrong side of this mini gang. They just walk around the problem not wanting to get involved. These parents usually would be the first to say after someone student shot up their school, why didn't someone recognize this problem beforehand.

"THE START OF WAR"

An announcer on television was talking about one of the oldest books on war. The cadets in all branches of the armed services studied these principles even today. Sun Tzu's *The Art of War* grew in popularity and saw practical use in Western society, and his work has continued to influence culture and politics ever since. It was first written somewhere around 722-481 BC. What I intended to get, if anything, from the book was concepts of battle. Whether it was one against one or one against a million I felt there might be something in there I could use.

There were two points the book made out to be most important: by positioning yourself on the high ground before a battle you have a distinct advantage and any information about your enemy was as useful as any weapon. So remembering the lawnmower incident, I started questioning Barbara on what else had happened all the years she lived there before I arrived at the house.

I also loved playing chess and had read many books on chess strategic concepts. One key strategy was to set a trap. I felt this would prove essential in my long-term objectives.

The high ground in our case would mean not playing dirty. I wanted to take a high moral ground. I did not want to do anything illegal although it would have been easy.

It was getting a little scary because as time went on, they were getting more aggressive. They had already proven that they would do things that I never knew neighbors could be capable of. They had the type of mindset that allowed them to do things I had previously thought unimaginable and they had to be stopped.

It seemed that no one actually believed the stories about our neighbors doing the things they were doing. I needed solid proof that they were in fact attacking me and my wife on a continued basis. I would need to set several traps for them. I knew they would lie or present false evidence to incriminate us but I would not drop down to use his underhanded methods. They were just not worth getting in trouble with the law. Besides, Barbara and I were not that type of people.

I began almost immediately to accumulate knowledge of tactics they used in their attempts to make Anna's life miserable. Barbara knew the history of Rudy and Bulla's war with Anna, and said they knew and used many of the city codes to harass her whenever possible. Barbara had the city codes book marked on her computer and showed me how to access this information.

For Rudy and Bulla, calling the police was one of the favorite sources of harassing their neighbors. On paper their calls made them look like the victims rather than the ones doing the harassing. They would never sign the complaints. Therefore, they could not be held liable if the police reports proved to be false. This was a tactic of theirs to keep their opponent off balance.

They would use their age as senior citizens to appear helpless and unable to defend themselves. Barbara told of an advocate service for senior citizens that they used all the time. I asked her what that service could do.

There are a group of attorneys who are paid by our taxes to protect the elderly. They could do plenty for Rudy because they believed Rudy's complaints. Thelma, who headed the service, could get nasty and start calling us to court to defend ourselves if she wanted to. She had our landlord Fred's telephone number and had already called many times complaining to him about Barbara. He knew all about Rudy and Bulla's sociopathic behavior and for the most part he disregarded it all. Fred was getting up in his years and really did not want to be harassed with the city calling him, along with the crazy neighbors.

I did not certainly start any of these confrontations; I was just on the defensive side of things. I was operating in a manner of defense rather than any sort of aggressiveness. It would be time consuming as well as expensive if we had to hire attorneys to go to court. If their attorney got nasty with having a tight relationship with the city she could call in city inspectors to check the house for any electrical, plumbing, or code violations. Then they would call the owner and he would blame us for fighting with Rudy. We would look like the troublemakers.

"They know very dirty tricks and have no reservations about using them."

"They can't get us thrown out of this house. Barbara, you do have a lease, don't you?"

"Not since my husband died. Fred has been so good to me. After Daniel died I could not pay the rent. After paying all the medical bills I just ran out of money. He let me stay here for six months when I could not pay the rent. So ever since then I never bothered with a lease, nor did I ever complain about anything that would bother him."

"Did you ever pay him for those six back months' rent?"

"Yes. I took in a roommate and saved like crazy and finally gave him every penny."

"Well, Barbara, now that I'm living here we have to have a lease and I want my name on it."

Barbara did not want to call, I could tell. One week went by. She hadn't called. I asked her again to call but she balked again. After week three I put it to her to call him or give me his telephone number and I would call. Three days later she got a hold of him. He said that he would not put my name on the lease but would put Barbara's name on the lease. He did not know me, I was the new tenant, but it still sounded a bit strange.

I asked Barbara, "Does Rudy have our landlord's telephone number?"

"Yes, he does."

"Well, he must have called him complaining about me. Why else would the landlord not want another name on the lease?"

"He calls him all the time. Fred hates them. He knows about their tricks, yet he really does not want to be bothered by them. So if we want to stay here we have to keep things kind of quiet."

Without my name on the lease my rights as a tenant were somewhat gray to me. He did send Barbara an unsigned lease agreement for three years without my name on it. In one way it was okay with us. Without a yearly lease we could move out with little or no notice. We were living on a month-to-month lease agreement.

Barbara added Thomas Smith to the lease and initialed it. I told her not to sign it first. We did not think he would sign it, yet we felt that he may change his mind if things cooled down around the house. He could actually not look at it before signing it. He told us he was not going to deal with the lease until the spring. He was waiting for the time to pass to see if things calmed down. I was really getting tired of being the bad person when in reality I had done nothing to anyone. Who knew what could happen by the spring. Nevertheless, he went to the south for the winter and told Barbara he would look it over when he returned in the spring. There was nothing further we could do and just let it go. We mailed the lease back to him with my name added, unsigned, and left it up to him. I told Barbara that I would really have to think hard about living there without my name on the lease.

We then just continued with our lives. We never heard a word about the lease from him. It was put on hold. I was not okay with this and would pick back up on it in the spring. He would not dare throw us out in the winter; it would be too hard for him to find another renter.

The winter was somewhat of a reprieve from Rudy and Bulla. It kept both of us in our houses much more than in the spring. The war was still on, but the frequency of the incidents of confrontation was reduced.

PLOWED

January came and one day when we were both at work it snowed some nineteen inches or more. We could not pull our cars into the driveway. It was just too much snow for me and her to shovel. I knew a young person who did some winter plowing, so I gave David a call. He said he could make it out the next day at 5:00 p.m. I wanted to be home in case Rudy tried to make trouble.

I was watching the news and heard the truck pulling into the driveway, so I grabbed my coat and went outside. Barbara was right behind me. As we expected, there came Rudy outside as well. Barbara knew the city code for snow placement and so did David. He had his girlfriend with him. I guessed they were going to attend a wedding or some dressy event after plowing. David wore a black beret, with a long black over coat.

The black truck was new with a new plow. David began to plow, dragging the snow out of our driveway and placing it on Rudy's parkway. This was the legal place according to city code. Rudy stood close to the property line and stared at David in the same creepy way he always stared at Barbara and me. After a few passes David stopped the truck. He got out of the truck, walked up to Rudy and asked him, "What is your problem?"

Now this was someone young who looked as though he spent his free time in the gym. David had a serious look on his face and a very serious tone to his voice.

Rudy replied, "I don't have a problem." Rudy stayed for two more passes of the plow and like the bully in the schoolyard whose bluff was called Rudy ran back in his house. Barbara and I just smiled and went in the house to get warm. She was giggling in the kitchen.

It remained cold for weeks and I enjoyed seeing all that snow piled on Rudy's parkway. The whole scene of David getting out of the truck and confronting Rudy gave us a chuckle whenever we brought back the memory.

For the rest of the winter we did not see much of our neighbors, but Rudy still found ways to attack us. It seemed to have become his life's work to mess with us whenever he could think of something horrible to do.

I was in the basement. The house was quiet, and I heard the water running. I looked around and didn't see anything, so I followed the sound. It was coming from a faucet in the back of the house. I threw on a coat and went out back to find that the outside water faucet had been turned on. It was not turned on full stream but enough was coming out that if I did not stop it in a timely manner the water could cause significant damage to the yard and the house. The backyard was flooding and freezing, so I grabbed a wrench and went out to give it a good tightening.

Could I turn it on and just not turn it off tightly? Could a raccoon somehow have been smart enough to turn it on?

I mentioned it to Barbara and she gave me a surprised response, "Damn it! Rudy knew we could not turn that faucet off from within the house because I overheard him and Daniel my late husband discussing it one day. Thomas, that jerk Rudy turned it on."

I had to do something; I needed to catch him in the act. I hooked up a camera and hid it from plain sight. I was able to record six hours at a time. It was easy to set my trap. I simply would run down to the basement and press start in the morning before work. It would rewind automatically when the tape ended. If the water were not running I wouldn't need to check the tape.

It was time to tell Barbara what I was up to.

"Barbara, something strange is happening."

"What now?"

"The faucet that is located just under the kitchen window. Someone has been turning it on. Got any idea who would do such a thing?"

"That would be Rudy"

I knew it would be Rudy but I wanted to check to find out why she was being so sure it was him.

"Rudy? How's that?

"Rudy knows we cannot shut it off for the winter from the inside. I remember him and my husband discussing it years ago. No animal could turn it on but that big rat that lives next door sure could."

Three weeks passed and then I saw human footprints in the snow. The water had not been turned on. I wanted to see who, during the time we were at work, was in our back yard. I viewed the tape and observed a utility man walking through the backyard; I guessed he was reading meters. Two weeks later, the snow had melted; I was in the basement and heard the water running. This time I knew where it was coming from. I went out and sure enough, it was running again, this time stronger than last time. This time the backyard was quite flooded. I got a bigger plumber's wrench and tightened it as much as possible. Someone, a person, was turning that water on. I almost ran to the basement. My heart was pumping. I put tape on fast forward until I saw movement. I stopped the tape, rewound and played it at normal speed. There Rudy was, unaware of the camera, and doing his dirty work. I called for Barbara to come downstairs to view the tape.

"Oh boy, I could call the police and have him arrested."

"Thomas, think about this for one minute. Our place is vulnerable to them all day long. The law will just give him a slap on the wrist and next time he will just be more careful. He has nothing better to do except think of things to do to us. Five days a week we go to work."

"You are right Barbara, it is just a minor incident. I need much more tape on this guy. I am sure he will provide us with much more if we just are patient. When I bust him I want to show the authorities that this was not just a onetime event but an ongoing constant attack. Call the landlord and tell him that the faucet in the back is leaking and we need a plumber to replace the valve with one we can shut off from the inside."

"Damn Rudy. Thomas, he is just getting crazier all the time. Yes, I will call the landlord and tell him what is happening. If he keeps getting all this aggravation he may ask us to leave. We will not be able to find a place as nice as this for so little money. I have lived here so long and don't want to move. I don't want to give them the satisfaction of running us off either."

"Oh, hell. I will call the plumber. I will pay to have it done. It should only cost a couple of hundred to have it done."

"No, we are not going to pay for something Rudy did. I will call the landlord tomorrow; he is good about fixing anything that goes wrong with the house."

"Barbara, you know I'm very creative. It is just a question of where he will attack next, so I can position the cameras to catch him in the act, again without his knowledge."

"He will catch you putting up them."

"Well, it looks like I will have to be extra cautious."

"Did you say cameras? How many are you going to use? Don't do anything illegal. He is not worth it. You're the one who will get arrested."

"I told you, I won't do anything illegal."

"Thank you, Thomas. I don't want to have to move."

Barbara called the landlord and as she predicted he called a plumbing company and they promptly installed a shut off valve inside so that our running water problem was controlled.

At this point in time I needed him to further incriminate himself. I had the camera up and had more cameras coming. I talked to a friend of mine who is an attorney. He said I could get an order of no trespassing. So I brought the idea for discussion with Barbara.

"Barbara, I talked to a friend of mine who is an attorney. He told me to call the police giving them instruction to deliver to Rudy an order of no trespassing on our property."

"Can we do that?"

"Yes, we can. Is it okay with you?"

"Go for it."

I went to the police station and waited for forty-five minutes. An officer finally came out to see me. I explained to the officer that I was having much trouble with Bulla and Rudy and my attorney advised me to ask the police to put an order to them of no trespassing on our grounds. Could I prevent him from trespassing on our grounds?

"Yes, but understand that you cannot go on his land either," the officer said.

"No problem. I never go there or want to."

"Mr. Smith, we know about Rudy. We are sorry, but there is not much we can do. We will order him today to stay off your grounds."

I thanked the officer. To have that restriction on them felt good. we would finally have some protection. I could not wait to tell Barbara, so I called her on my cell as soon as I got to the car.

"Hi, honey, I went to the police station and talked to Officer Adamik. I explained our situation. He commented that the city police have had many confrontations with this couple and would tell Rudy and Bulla they are not to set one foot on our land."

"You know, now you have started a full-blown war."

"We didn't start it. They have been at it for a while now. I'm just starting to fight back. I'm sick of just taking it, sick of hoping for a miracle that they suddenly turn into born again Christians. That is never going to happen. They are evil, mean, and crazy. We can't just roll over and take everything they throw at us. Those crazies are starting to escalate their aggression. We must do what we can to protect ourselves."

"Okay Thomas. Just don't lose your temper if something happens."

"Barbara, I have seen you lose your temper. Don't you get thrown in jail either? I haven't done anything illegal and do not intend to. I believe I'm smart enough to fight fair while showing them there will be consequences for their aggression. Oh, and by the way, I will order a land survey to determine exactly where the property line is between our houses. Is this okay with you, Barbara?"

"Okay When are you going to have them come out?"

"I will have them come on a Monday. I want to be here when they come. I will have them drive stakes in so that we know exactly what ground they can and cannot stand on. I have been looking at the property and I think they have some flowers planted on our side of the driveway. I won't know until we get the survey."

I could tell that Barbara was starting to get really nervous and worried but I knew a part of her was a fierce combatant. I believe we were finally feeling empowered. I had shown Barbara that even though we were renters we had rights and just did not have to take their abuse. We could fight back.

Our front porch had windows all around. We had a big couch that Barbara and I, and sometimes the whole family, which included the dog and cat, would sit on. We had no children, so we considered our animals our family. We all would look out the front window to people-watch, when any of our good neighbors would walk by. We were friendly and waved to the passersby. They always returned our waves. We loved to just sit there and look out.

Bulla and Rudy had the same kind of porch. The window of their porch was about fifty feet from ours. They had slatted blinds that they never opened. Whenever Barbara would go out on the porch she would see the blinds separate on Bulla's porch, and two black eyes would peek at her. Barbara supposed that Bulla thought that she couldn't be seen peeking but Barbara could always see the blinds separate.

One day when Barbara caught her peeking she just waved at her. Bulla quickly let go of the blinds and they snapped shut. This ritual became an automatic response. Bulla would peek, Barbara would wave, and the blinds would snap closed. We found it ridiculously amusing. What they wanted was to try to make us uncomfortable by having someone watch our every move. It really did not bother us very much. As time went by we just learned to live this way. While consciously it was no big deal, subconsciously it had to be stirring emotions of violation.

One day I went to look for the definition of bullying:

"A person is bullied when he or she is exposed, repeatedly and over time, to negative actions on the part of one or more other persons, and he or she has difficulty defending him or herself."

That definition suited Barbara and I perfectly.

Mostly we think that children on the playground are the bullies, not senior citizens, but the senior citizen could be even meaner than the young could and could cause even greater harm to their victims. We were left to deal with our living situation and the only option I felt we had was to fight back.

Coming home from work, I pulled into the driveway and Rudy was standing not in our driveway but he was as close to it as he could be without trespassing. He was there, just staring at me. I got out of the car and walked up to him. Looking him in the eyes I asked him.

"Why, are you like this? Why are you doing the mean things you do?"

His answer was conversation ending: *"This is how I get my jollies."*

FRIENDLY ADVICE
COULD BE DANGEROUS

I have many friends. Some I talk to once a month, others I talk to every couple of days, and others fall somewhere in between. They listen to me complain. What are friends for anyway? I listen to them complaining about how life has wronged them as well.

It is always entertaining to get their views on my problems and to hear their solutions. From the time I moved in with Barbara I would disclose the latest event that was taking place between us and Bulla and Rudy. They loved those names. They seemed to fit the characters in the stories I was sharing with them. After a while my friends were very anxious to hear the latest outrageous very bad neighbor story. They seemed to be fascinated by their creativity. In fact, they were more interested in finding out what problems I was having than discussing their problems. It was therapeutic to have so many good friends that I could vent my frustration to.

My friends would come up with outrageous revenge plots all of which, of course, were illegal. They all were all quite brave as long as it was me risking bodily harm or jail and not them living next to the whack jobs. Sometimes they would come up with some very creative revenge plots. I would not consider doing anything illegal but talk is cheap entertainment and they were full of ideas. Listening to their creativity was good entertainment. One suggested that I go to such extreme measures that there would be no retaliation. I told them in an earlier conversation that there was nothing I could do that would stop these two. Teddy suggested that I buy some M80's fireworks and tape them to all his windows using slow-burning cigarettes. Then I would light the cigarettes and go bowling. It would take twenty minutes for the cigarettes to burn down to ignite the M80's which should blow out the windows.

"Gee, Teddy, that's just great. After that do you suggest I get two automatic remote starters for my two cars?"

Teddy laughed saying, "After you did that he would be so afraid he wouldn't do anything."

I told Teddy, "I am not dealing with rational people. Forget about it. That was very creative but you are an idiot."

He said, "Thank you."

My friend Bobby had a truck and did some snowplowing in the winter. He wanted to plow Rudy's driveway in with ten feet of snow at two o'clock in the morning. I pictured Rudy coming out in the morning, looking at all that snow, and going absolutely bonkers. I would have really gotten a kick out of that one if I let him do it but I said no to his generous offer.

Men just talk sometimes just to sound tough. One of my friends wanted to tie him to a chair in the basement and work him over until we were sure he was cured. Of course, that would be kidnapping, attempted murder, and torture. I am sure I would come out of it with a sentence of life in prison. I have to get some smarter friends.

Then there were the childish ones like gathering dog poop, putting it in a paper bag, setting the bag on fire and filming him coming out of the house to stomp out the fire. I could super-glue all the house doors and car locks, buy skunk-smelling liquid to pour in the air intake of the automobile, or put finger-nail polish remover on the car which would remove the paint overnight. It seemed they would think all week of ways to get even, most of which would land me in a cell. Many of my friends' ideas were just too ridiculous to repeat. It seemed that they were getting madder than me at these people and they did not have to live next to them.

The first part of any of my conversations with my friends would start off with them asking me a question: "Well, what have they done lately?" I would oblige them with details of the latest attack. They all had something in common with their reply to the stories: they said that they would not take it. I tried to explain that if they were in my spot they would soon find out that there was very little they could do.

Most of them said, "I wouldn't take it from those two. There should be something you could do to stop them."

Looking from the outside in was easy. I tried to tell them that any action I took would be a disaster for me. Rudy had no respect for the law and knew his way around it. He has been playing this game for many years with his other neighbor and I was just the new victim on the block. He was constantly saying or just doing things to cause trouble. He dared me repeatedly to do something to them. In fact, he wanted us to so that he could call the police with a legitimate complaint. He would stand on the edge of his property and call us over to insult us in the hope that we would react in a negative manner or just touch him, anything that he could use as an excuse to call the police. He would send the police over to our house on a regular basis with made up complaints about us. The police would show up and ask us about their complaint. We had to explain away their ridiculous complaints on a regular basis and that meant constant trouble.

Thinking about revenge and actually taking action and doing something ugly were two different things. I had been fighting back, doing what I could do. I had animals at home alone and no one watched the house all day long when we were at work. I had to come up with something that would work under those restrictive circumstances. I was sure that I would come up with something soon that could stop him. We would not put it past them to hurt our children, the ones with four paws.

Because of their war with the other neighbor, who also was retired, Bulla and Rudy would never leave the house unguarded. If it were necessary for the both of them to be out of the house at the same time they would hire a guard to watch the house. The guard would sit in on the front porch, peeking out the blinds every now and then, looking for any possible intruders.

Several years ago, well before I moved in, Barbara saw Bulla crawling out of a basement window. The window was on our side of the house. This was one of the few times Barbara was on speaking terms with Bulla and she just had to find out what was going on.

"Bulla, what are you doing? Is everything okay? Are you all right?"

"Oh, yes. Rudy's not home and I just have to go to the store but I do not want Anna to see me leave the house."

Bulla told Barbara that crazy Anna put grease in her potted plants. She was in a hurry, so she did not get into the details or the reason why Anna did that. Barbara asked Anna about it later but just got the brush off.

Bulla asked Barbara, "Do you mind if I walk around the back of your house where Anna cannot see me leave?"

Barbara just looked at her and paused for a moment to let what Bulla said to settle in.

"Sure you can, Bulla."

These memories would come to Barbara every now and then. I had asked her to inform me of this type of strange behaviors whenever she could remember such stories. According to the *"The Art of War," information* on the enemy was not only important to defending ourselves but also necessary to win the war.

The more of these bizarre stories Barbara related to me, the more concerned I became. I was beginning to think that they might have had something in their house that was making them so crazy: a gas leak, mold, or radon gas. Something was wrong there. Normal people just did not act or think this way. They ate food from their garden. They might have been ingesting something. If it were just one of them I would think it more of a medical problem. To have both of them acting like teenage bullies was just strange.

I asked Barbara about her late husband Daniel. "How did you and he get along with them?"

"We had periods of peace and civil behavior. If we made any kind of mistake it would take them a long time before they could forget about it."

"How long before they would forget about it?"

"They would not let it go for a very long time."

"What could be considered a mistake?"

"Well, a shovel of snow thrown on their property (like you did) would be good enough for several months' retaliation."

"No way."

THE ZUCCHINI IS DEAD

I asked Barbara, "Can you remember one big thing that set them off with you and Daniel?"

She thought for a while and told me about a time when they were actually getting along with them. Rudy's back fence was falling down and he needed another man to help repair the fence properly. Even though he knew, Daniel had cancer and kidney failure. Rudy came across the driveway. He had seen Daniel through the window.

He yelled out to Daniel, "Hey, Daniel, could you give me a hand to set the fence in the backyard in place?"

Daniel was sick, yet he said, "Okay, sure. I will be right back there."

Barbara told him, "Just lie down and I will tell Rudy you are not feeling well."

Daniel said to her, "No, it is okay. I am not feeling that bad. I'm just a little dizzy. It should only take a few minutes and then we will have it done. We are finally on peaceful terms. I don't want them to think we are not being neighborly. Just let me do this for them."

Barbara followed Daniel out to watch him and Bulla came out of her house to watch as well. The fence was heavy. Daniel picked up his end to place the fence in its pre-determined spot but he lost his balance. The fence pushed Daniel, causing him to stumble backward. In order not to hurt himself he threw the fence forward while taking a big step backward to get his legs and feet under himself. His left foot landed in her zucchini patch. His other foot followed, stomping on one large, ready-to-be-harvested, zucchini. You would have thought that Daniel had just stomped their dog dead. Bulla's body was tense as she began taking quick little steps to gain a better look at the damage Daniel's foot had done.

She started screeching at Daniel, "You're crushing a zucchini. Stop moving around and just get out of the garden. Can't you see what you're doing?"

Then her voice became even louder. "Damn fool, just get out of the damn garden."

Daniel did not say anything. He just walked out of the garden taking in the over-the-top verbal lashing he had just received. One damaged zucchini for all that screeching. The cherry bomb on top of the cake was Rudy saying to Daniel, "Get the hell off my land."

Daniel was not feeling well and the event left both of them speechless. They simply turned and walked back to the house.

Daniel said, "So much for helping the neighbors."

Barbara wanted to say, "I told you not to go out to help him," but it was just not the right time or the right thing to say. Hell, Daniel was just trying to be a nice person and help a neighbor. Instead he got a verbal lashing and was thrown off their property.

"What did Daniel do?"

"He was sick and really couldn't do much. He had cancer."

"Did they know he had cancer?"

"Yes. There was one time they did something crueler and more unbelievable."

"Tell me. I can't imagine anything worse."

"We went shopping, parked in the driveway, and began to bring the groceries back in the house. This was after the zucchini incident. Bulla and Rudy were standing on the parkway watching us. Daniel was walking a bit off gait, which caught their attention. He lost his balance, tripping on the last step, and fell through the screen door."

"What did they do? Did they call 911? Did they come over to help?"

"Thomas, I know this is hard to believe but they started to laugh! I guess they were thinking that since he stepped on their zucchini it was his proper due."

"That is just evil. What about you, Barbara? How did this affect you?"

"I think that all the stress of their unreasonable behavior and my husband becoming ill had taken its toll. I knew from experience that they were going to remain nasty and get even nastier as time went on. I was not feeling good. I took my blood pressure and saw it was way up. I called my doctor and she told me to take my pressure twice a day for five days. I had my own blood pressure machine at home. I took my pressure twice a day. I religiously took my pressure, once in the morning and once just before dinner. I had my numbers and went to see the doctor. She wrote me another prescription. I was instructed to take the medication for two weeks and then call her.

It took the doctor several months to figure out what to have me take. I finally got my medication right and got my blood pressure under control. The doctor said I could have died. With regular doctor visits and careful monitoring of my medication it seems to be under control now.

"This is part of the reason why I'm always telling you not to start anything with them."

Barbara told me some of the other bizarre things Bulla would do.

"One day I was looking out the front porch window and I observed Bulla sifting through my garbage."

"What in the world was she looking for?"

"Not sure. My friend Sally was over that day and had witnessed her sifting through my garbage. Sally got very angry, so she opened the door and yelled out. "Hey you, bag lady, get away from that garbage. If you eat that it will just get you sick."

This was just another day of bizarre behavior to Barbara. On more than one occasion Bulla, who did not like Sally, would yell out obscenities like, "You're nothing but a big fat whore," or, her favorite, "Trailer trash whore." Sally took special pleasure in telling Bulla not to eat the garbage.

My thoughts churned. I had to protect her from the present while not forgetting what they had done to her in the past. I wished Barbara would agree to us moving into another house. Like Anna on the other side of them,

Barbara refused to give in to them and give them the satisfaction of having made us move out.

I asked Barbara to recount some other events that took place before I arrived. That seemed to open Barbara's memory and she told me that once they accused her of running a whorehouse. They called the police saying that men were coming and going all night long. They said they had seen the whores; a couple of young women in the house dressed in short skirts with their boobs hanging almost out of their blouses. They told the police that they had to stop this whoring immediately. A police officer banged on the door. Barbara answered and asked what was wrong. The officer had been to her house before for some other bogus complaint that Rudy and Bulla had drummed up.

He said, "It seems that your neighbor thinks you are running a whorehouse with men coming and going all night long." After the words came out of his mouth Barbara could tell that he was trying hard not to laugh.

She asked the officer to come in and they sat on the front porch while she explained that at her job they hired college students to work for the school year. On school break she usually invited some of the student workers over for dinner or just to visit. The two girls who were there worked for her all right but not as hookers. One of the boys who came over worked for her as well and the other two boys were just friends of the students. She knew them all from work and there was no whoring going on. Barbara told him she did not understand how they could show up there on some bogus report of a whorehouse operating in the middle of a block of single-family homes in a middle-class neighborhood.

"Isn't there a limit to how many times they can call you with nothing ever coming out of it?"

"We are very sorry, but the answer is no. As many times as they call we must investigate. There is no limit. Try to have a good night. Sorry to have bothered you."

The officer had a sympathetic look on his face and Barbara could tell he was sincere in his apology. He was looking down when he walked back to his squad car. He didn't bother to report to Bulla and Rudy. Barbara could tell he was deep in thought and she assumed he was trying to figure out some way to stop this madness.

That night Barbara took her blood pressure and of course it was dangerously high. She explained to her workers what had happened and why the police were talking to her on the porch. At first they laughed for a while but then they got mad. Barbara had to talk them down from going over there and confronting them. "Bulla and Rudy would use that circumstance to make up some lie about you saying or doing something illegal and they would just call the police again, so please just let it go."

The next day Barbara went to the police station to talk to the officer who came over the night before. She explained her medical condition to him and told him that such a horrible complaint caused her blood pressure to rise to a dangerous level. She told him she could have a stroke, with the number that high.

He tried to comfort her. "Barbara, we know about them. Practically all the officers in this town know about them. If it happens again please do not take it to heart. Just try to chalk it up to some paranoid older people who just don't get a lot of things right."

His explanation of the situation did not make her feel a whole lot better. From then on, when she had guests over, she would explain that the police might be coming over to chat later on that night. She made a joke out of their antics to her guests and everyone found it curiously amusing.

"Well, Barbara, I cannot promise you that I am going just to sit by idly and take that abuse. Call your doctor and get an appointment to see her to get some stronger meds. It looks like you will need them. I'm sure they have moved their attention to me, so, from now on, let them be my problem. Just don't let yourself get upset. It's all just nonsense anyway. If you let them upset you, they win."

She nodded her head. I didn't know if she could stop from feeling but I guessed probably not. I would try to take on as much of their attention as possible keeping her out of the direct line of fire.

One night I was lying in bed and I thought of using technology. The next day I went online to buy more of the security cameras. In order to see the whole house I would need about four more cameras.

It took a couple of days. After some research I found a place that sold security equipment. I went there on my day off and found out that for a couple of hundred dollars I could buy the equipment necessary to set up five cameras to capture what went on at the house while we were at work. I would have to set them up without Bulla and Rudy seeing me so I could catch them doing illegal things. Trespassing would be a little infraction of the law. I needed much more, like him stealing things out of the shed or whatever they did to our house while we were at work. Being able to see what was going on while we were at work could really be fun but I had to be careful. If he caught me setting the cameras up my sting would be ruined.

The cameras would give us the peace of mind so that we could leave the house. That would be good enough for me to actually coexist with these maniacs. I wanted to get enough footage on Rudy that he would be arrested and severely punished.

The cameras were in black and white but they had the ability to film in the dark with just a small amount of light. The longest tape you could buy would last for six hours. Between Barbara and me, we had five cameras that worked by staggering the automatic on times so I could take many hours of coverage, protecting the house from any abuse.

When I told Barbara of my plan she was worried about any unknown consequence that may occur from my actions. I consoled her by telling her it was just a protection tool that we could use. She thought I was a bit out there for ordering the equipment and setting my traps but I had made her aware of the fact that they could be dangerous. I told her to remember the lawnmower. She took a couple of days and then said it was okay for me to put my plan into action. She did say that they would catch me right away. To me that meant game on. I just had to be extra careful in placing the cameras.

The more tapes I had of them doing their evil deeds the greater chance there was that the law would punish them to teach them the lesson that there would be consequences for their actions. I would continue to gather as much evidence as I could to show the authorities. I was sure they would just love to bust them for all the aggravation they caused the police through the years. They were vigilant in watching our every move. They had blinds on all their windows but we could sometimes see them watching. I could not for sure tell all the time but I would have to go under the assumption that they were always watching.

GOING TO THE MOVIES

S pring had arrived. The cameras and all the new equipment were purchased and everything was tested and found to be working well. I had to be careful that they would not see inside our house exposing the sting. I shut our blinds so that they would not see inside our house but I knew this would put them on extra alert of something going on. I thought this would be easy but I soon found out that the concealment of the cameras would be a bigger problem than I had originally thought. They may catch me; I just hoped that I could get enough incriminating footage on them before the cameras were discovered.

I must admit this was exciting for me. I started with one camera concealed in a stuffed animal on our front porch, looking out on the front lawn. On our front lawn there was one patch of grass that would always turn brown. I had put down new seed many times but it always turned brown while all the surrounding grass stayed green. It was a true mystery. On a hunch, I turned the first camera on that patch of brown grass. It was unnatural that one patch would turn brown while all the other grass was doing fine. I had a hunch about some foul play.

The porch had windows all around. I placed the stuffed animal on the upper portion of the couch looking outside. I placed the camera at night. The installation went unnoticed. I was taking every precaution not to be caught. I set the VCR to run for six hours from 9:00 a.m. until 3:00 p.m. I could watch on fast-forward, so it took about twenty minutes to view the entire tape. I set it and let it run. I could not wait to finish work to watch the tape.

When I got home from work the tape had finished running and automatically rewound. I turned it on, set it on fast-forward and waited to see if I had caught anything in my trap.

It was not long before I observed a person on our front lawn. My heart began to pound a little stronger as I rewound the tape to view it at normal speed. Sure enough, it was Bulla. She brought her dog to pee on our front lawn. I thought that she may have seen the camera because she looked right into the front porch window with a look of defiance on her face. The dog finished and she left the viewing screen. Had to rewind the tape and play it several times. It was a believe-it-or-not experience. I had caught her in my trap. Man, this was good. It was a small thing but a terrific start to my plan. I had him turning on the faucet in the backyard and now her dragging her dog over to pee on our front lawn.

Barbara was coming home in one hour and I could hardly wait to show her what I had caught on tape. Time went slowly as I waited for her and I amused myself by watching the tape several times over. The look of defiance on Bulla's face was comical.

Barbara came home at her normal time. I was sitting on the couch in front of the TV with the remote in my hand. Immediately she asked, "Well, did you get anything on tape?"

"Yep. Wait till you see this. You know that brown spot on our front lawn where the grass won't grow green? The tape will show you why that occurs."

"What? What did you get on tape?"

"Sit down and watch this. I'm not sure if she saw the camera or not."

I ran the tape and showed it to Barbara. I was happy that I had finally recorded this on tape for the world to see what evil looked like. Was this just an aberration or would she do it again tomorrow? Did she see the camera?

Just then Barbara poured a little cold water on my exuberance. "Thomas, in our town dogs can pee legally anywhere. It is not against the law."

"Yes, but it shows such intent on her part to cause stressful mental harm and damage to property. Have you forgotten about the no trespass order we have on them?"

"Quit being dramatic, I'm telling you in our town a dog can pee anywhere legally, end of story."

"Yes, the dog can pee legally but the owner purposely bringing the dog over to damage their neighbors' property is a different crime. It is not the end. It is the just beginning of the story and I want to see her do it again tomorrow. One little trespassing is nothing but wait till I'm done collecting all my evidence."

The next day I set the recorder to start taping when I left for work and I turned it off when I got home. I fast-forwarded the tape and again I saw Bulla bring that dog over to my lawn to pee in the exact same spot. She had that same defiant look on her face. She had trained that dog to pee there. Barbara came home and I told her that she had done it again.

She said, "So what? We have very little."

I began to plan to set up the rest of the cameras. One would be in the shed. What could I put in there that would make Rudy's mouth water? Bulla hated fertilizers or insect-killers, so I decided to buy a new spreader that would hold a five-pound bag of grub-killer. I would make sure she saw me spreading the grub killer close to her property but not on her property. I would make sure she saw the bag of grub-killer and the green tub that held the grub-killer. I would use the wheeled spreader and then put it in the shed. The plan was that Bulla would command Rudy to make it disappear. I did not know if my trap would work but it was worth a try. That would be a stolen property offense and another trespassing.

Putting the camera in the shed was not easy. I camouflaged it as much as possible to avoid detection. I actually drilled a small hole in the house to hide the wires going to the VCR. Every morning I would turn it on and collect six hours of footage to view. I did not need to check the tape. All I had to do was check the shed if anything was missing. I also had a fifteen-pound red metal vice in the shed. This was a good tool that any handy man could use. I left it out on the shelf like a big red apple.

It took three weeks. I checked the shed every day, and at last there it was – or should I say, there it wasn't. I went directly to the VCR, hoping I did this right. Was it on? Did I rewind the tape? I began watching on fast-forward until I saw something. Then I rewound and held my breath. Bingo. Rudy went into the shed, picked up the red vise, and carried it out. I saw him check the driveway before quickly walking toward his shed.

This was sweet. I was sure there was no city ordinance for stealing the neighbor's vise. Rudy was a great liar and I assumed when confronted he would probably say he just borrowed it and forgot to return it. However, I had the tape and now I had proof of him taking it. I would make a police report about it missing. Then when he claimed he just borrowed it he would be caught in a lie. This was getting good; the chessboard was leaning in my favor. I had hoped that this could be a few days in jail and many hours of community service. This would be my hope. What would actually happen, I had no idea. All I knew was that I needed as much incriminating tape as possible.

I might have to get a little more daring in placing the cameras. Last summer something or someone had stomped our freshly planted mums, and I had a feeling that would happen again. This time I would catch them. I wanted to run the wire to the camera along the white gutter, so I painted the wires white for camouflage. I painted the camera white as well. This was going to be tricky. I wanted to mount the camera out of the rear bedroom window on the second floor of the house but I could not do this easily. Those eyes were ever vigilant.

I tried working in the dark and just found that impossible. Without any light I could not hang out the window and screw in the three mounting screws. I tried several times, only to drop six or seven screws. One time I almost fell out the window from the second floor. I would have to take a chance on first light on a Sunday before they woke up. The angle would also be tricky.

I got the camera installed on Sunday morning. I had begun work on it as soon as the sun rose enough in the sky for me to see. I messed with it until I captured the right angle down the driveway to the side of the house where the mums would be planted. This would be my new bait.

It was getting too light out and to prevent being observed I quickly disconnected the camera taking it inside. I did not want it detected before I had the chance to plant those mums. Leaving the camera exposed all week would be unnecessarily risky. I would have to wait another week to set the camera angle just right and then plant the pretty mums. Like chess and life, patience was necessary for success.

A week went by with nothing happening. At first light on the following Sunday I went back to work. I installed the camera and adjusted the proper angle for the camera. Then I went to the nursery for the pretty mums. We may have lost them last year due to Mother Nature. If we lost them again this year I would be able to see Mother Nature at work. Would some animal or man stomp them? Either way, if they were ill fated, I would have it on tape with my video recorder running.

THE STOMPER STOMPS

As a precautionary measure I told Barbara to call Fred and tell him of what we intended to do. The landlord knew of Rudy's antics...He gave us his blessing and actually said, "What a good idea."

This was a most worrisome wait. If he detected the camera, of course he would not stomp. Each day was not without anticipation and anxiety. Two and half weeks had passed and our mums were growing well. I was sure he'd stomped the mums the previous year. What was holding him up now was the question I was asking myself.

Mother Nature came to my rescue. One morning we had forty-five-mile-an-hour winds. Bulla's big pink-ball flowers had been large and healthy. The combination of rain and sun made growing conditions perfect. That day I noticed the flowers were so large the stems looked as though they were not strong enough to hold up the flowering part of the plant. They were bigger than a baseball but not as large as a softball. The heads of the flowers were drooping because of their size and a few of them broke the stems. These flowers were planted right next to where Barbara parked her car. I thought, "Those two, being paranoid about everything, will surely think we broke them." They would ignore the fact that we had high winds the day before and confidently blame us. Not that they needed it but I was sure that this would be cause for some sort of retaliation.

The Art of War proved to be true once again. Knowledge of your enemy is a most important weapon. On Monday, I double checked to make certain I had the camera angle right. When I came home from work on Tuesday my eyes trained on the mums. Our mums were planted on the passenger side of my car next to our house. I did not want to slow the car to look out the window at the mums. Rudy was outside at the back of his house on his property just staring at me when I pulled in the driveway. so I parked normally, stopping in my usual spot halfway down our driveway next to our house. I walked right by them giving the impression that I was not thinking of them and that I did not see them. I was perhaps deep in thought about work or something other than the mums. Without directly looking at them I observed that they were stomped but I did not let on that it really clicked in my mind. I went into the house and went to my VCR. Playing the tape on fast-forward I saw Rudy in the fast-moving frames. Was this tape going to be clear enough to see him stomping? I rewound and began playing forward. There it was. I got him plain as day. He stomped twice and then took a step backward to get a better look at his artwork before putting the final stomp to his creation.

Instead, I just bit my finger to deal with the emotion. As long as the camera was not discovered I was sure I could still gather more incriminating tape. I knew he had nothing better to do, so I was pretty sure he would come up with something as history showed me the mum stomping would not satisfy him. He would have to add to that.

A week later I turned the faucet on. Our new fifty-foot hose had transformed itself into a soaker hose. I turned on the water and started to sprinkle. The water hit me in the face. I jumped back and yelled aloud, "What the hell?" Upon closer examination, I noticed that it looked as though someone had taken an ice pick and punched a hole in the hose approximately every twelve to eighteen inches. This job looked as if it took a couple of hours to complete. I thought the vise he had stolen would a good tool for holding the hose while he punched the holes into it.

I wanted to see who was responsible for those holes, so I went to the VCR, rewound the tape, and played it. There was Rudy. He disengaged the hose and took it to his shed to work on. When he reappeared and reconnected the hose, it was turned into a soaker hose.

I shared my experiences with my friends. I could tell some of them may have thought I exaggerated when I told them the stories of the attacks on our house. I invited a few friends over for a barbecue and for entertainment I brought out mum stomping tape and the dog peeing tape. I also took the tape to work to show. Whenever I played it for friends it was amazing to watch them observe the tapes. Their faces showed a multitude of emotions: anger, amusement, horror, and sadness. This was reality TV at its finest.

Some would just start laughing and some would get very angry, jump up, and want to go after the individual. One friend wanted to go over to his house right then and confront Rudy. As a precautionary measure I made everyone I showed the tape to promise me not to go after this person. They thought that I was a little silly telling them that before they observed the tape. They were not that kind of people before I showed them the tape, yet after they had seen it, they were ready to fight. I assured them that I had a grand plan allowing me to get retribution for humanity. I told them not to worry; I would handle it in a legal way. I would be getting more tapes, solid proof of them causing us great distress.

Barbara had suffered great emotional distress over the years with all their cruelty. Her blood pressure had risen to dangerous levels during these attacks, all documented by her physician she was seeing at the time. All her doctors could attest to that. Barbara and I would never try to take the law into our own hands but I had a legal plan to attain retribution.

I had a collection of four tapes to show to the police to have Rudy and Bulla arrested. Having them arrested was fine but what then? I would be happy with him having to do jail time and probation would keep him from thinking about getting even. If I were the Judge I would make him do community service. He would have to do nice things for his neighbors: cut their grass, weed their flowerbeds, and remove the leaves, all the things both of them were so good at and loved to do. What took the anxiety out of going to work leaving the house unguarded was having the cameras. With the cameras in place, the house was protected. We could go to work knowing that if something bad happened they would be held accountable.

I got a little fussy and careless; I adjusted the angle of one of the cameras outside the upstairs bedroom. I should have known better. Rudy observed me making the adjustment and immediately realized that I had installed the cameras. Those days Barbara and I were walking around smiling now, and for sure, that must have looked different to them. Our relaxed demeanor told them something was different and really put them on guard.

"Barbara, I am pretty sure they discovered the cameras."

"What makes you say that?"

"I was out back and I looked at Rudy. He caught my eye and then looked right were the upstairs camera is."

"How many tapes do you have with incriminating evidence?"

"Let me think, Bulla bringing their dog to pee on the front lawn."

"I told you, not illegal."

"Yes, but trespassing is."

"Okay, what else do you have on tape?"

"I have tapes of Rudy turning on the water faucet in the backyard in the middle of winter. He did that twice. I have a tape showing him removing our hose and then bringing it back after turning it into a soaker hose. It also shows the red vise taken out of our shed. Oh, I almost forgot the stomping of the mums. The tapes will show malicious intent. They correspond with your medical condition really turning for the worse. I am hoping that we have as much as we need to put them in jail along with a huge civil suit."

"So this was your grand plan, your secret you did not want to tell anyone?"

"I hate to do this to you again Barbara, but it is only half of the grand plan. The second part is yet to come but I promise you it is just as delicious."

116

IT'S THE POLICE, DEAR,
IT'S OFFICER ADAMIK

The mums were stomped for the second time on a Tuesday. The police showed up that Tuesday night. I just happened to be looking out the front porch and saw a police squad car pull up. It was Barbara's old friend Officer Adamik. He first went to Rudy's house and then he came to our house. The nice officer rang the bell and Barbara arrived quickly, letting him in. The three of us sat on the porch to discuss why he had come over.

"It seems you had put up security cameras on your house that Bulla and Rudy object to. They called us to have you remove them. I told them that there was no law preventing you from having a security system. They are trying to say that you have the cameras pointed into their bed-room."

I was trying hard not to start laughing but I did anyway. The officer showed a slight smile. He looked embarrassed at the same time.

"Officer, I assure you they are not pointed anywhere at their house; they are only pointed at my grounds to protect us. When the cameras were put up I made sure not to show any windows of their house. I have a tape to show you, that I am sure will interest you. Do you have a minute? I will go get it and show it to you."

"Yes, go get it and take your time. I am not in a hurry."

I had the tapes all titled and I brought out the one called "Mum Stomper." Barbara asked if the officer would like some popcorn with his movie. He politely declined; he was still wearing his serious face. I turned on the VCR and pressed play. What came on the screen was a gray-haired man in our driveway, looking both ways up and down the street to make sure no person or car was coming and then walking up to the freshly planted mums and stomping them twice. He looked at his work and then stomped them a third time. He looked around again to make sure no one was looking and then returned to his house.

The officer said, "Would you like me to arrest him now?"

"Could I wait until a later date to have him arrested?"

"Yes, we could arrest him later."

Officer Adamik was disappointed in the decision to delay. Rudy and Bulla had been calling in bogus complaints for years as a means to harass their neighbors. The officer would have liked nothing better than make an arrest today. He told us to save the tape and call him anytime and he gave us his card.

When he left Barbara said, "What are you doing? Why didn't you show the officer all the tapes and have him arrested?"

"For what? Some misdemeanor offense? I want to talk to a criminal attorney first. They are guilty of much more than damage to property."

"You do have all those other tapes."

"Yes, I do, and I could have him brought up on charges tomorrow. His criminal acts go beyond mums being stomped. The tapes prove him guilty of destruction of property, theft, and trespassing. These acts caused you a great deal of pain and suffering. We must be careful; this is a legal matter. I want to obtain legal advice before pressing charges. Remember, I said I had a grand plan? We live in America; we have laws to protect us. Justice is not revenge. It is a word meaning bringing order to our society. I want to make a statement that shows all examples of bullying. These are to be discussed in public to show what harm it can do. I feel this needs expressing. You do not have to hit someone to cause severe damage to that person."

Whether the bully is in grammar school, middle school, high school, the workplace, or even some neighbors in their seventies, bullying is a hate crime and violators must be made aware of the harm they are doing. Rudy may have just stepped on some flowers but he did so much more harm. He wanted to cause pain; the emotional pain that associated with this type of ongoing assault is taxing on one's emotional state as my wife's blood pressure would attest to.

HERE COME THE LAWYERS

Now that the cameras were up and running, we had little to worry about. Even the bullies would not come over and do damage while being aware that their every move was being watched. Legally they could not step one foot on our property.

I asked Barbara, "Where is our property line exactly?"

"I do not know exactly where the line is."

"Well, since they are calling the police on us regularly now I think we need to know exactly where the property line is."

"How are you going to find that out?"

"I'm going to call and have the property surveyed. They will plant stakes with flags on the four corners. I have a feeling that Rudy's garden might be on our property at the end of the driveway."

"Oh my God, Thomas, order the survey."

We began to smile. We both were beginning to feel empowered.

I ordered the survey for Monday morning at ten o'clock. Monday came and the doorbell rang at ten twenty. He said, "I'm Gary."

I said, "I'm Thomas. Thanks for giving me the heads up that you are here. I want to observe you doing this."

We both walked back to his truck and he gathered some paperwork and the tripod. We headed out to place the first stake and Bulla came running out of her house to see what we were doing. She was walking quickly with paper and pen in hand, two deep lines separating her brow, the corners of her mouth turned way down. She was writing down the telephone number and the name of the company of his truck. She asked him, "Who ordered the survey?"

Before I could stop him from answering, he looked at his papers and said, "Thomas Smith."

I said, "Gary, for who are you working, her or me?"

"Of course I'm working for you."

"Then why are you answering her questions?"

"Well, she just asked me a simple question."

"She has no right asking you any questions. She is not paying you. I am paying you and I am telling you not to answer any more of her questions unless you do not want this job."

He reluctantly said, "All right."

Bulla realized there would be no more conversation with Gary. In a huff she spun around and went back in her house. Gary planted the second stake at the back of our lot, defining the property line. I was right; Rudy had planted part of his garden on our land. I had Gary pound another stake in the ground twenty-five feet from the back of the lot. This stake would clearly show that he was encroaching on our lot. I thought about digging up his garden on our land but decided just to leave it as a temptation for him to cross the line. Because of the trespass restriction he could look but not touch.

Barbara looked at the string and the two stakes in the ground and said, "Nothing like making the crazy guy mad."

Saturday and Sunday came and went. We did not even see Bulla or Rudy. Monday and then Tuesday came; it was cloudy and looked it might rain. Cold, damp, just an unpleasant day that put everyone in a foul mood. Barbara came home at her usual time. She had a look on her face that matched the weather.

"What's up, honey?"

"I received a telephone call today at work that proved to be most upsetting."

"From whom?"

"The city attorney."

"What? What in the world did they want with you?"

"Not me, exactly. Thelma wanted you."

"Who is Thelma?"

"An attorney for the city called Thelma and she said we must take down the cameras. She said we had them pointed at their bedroom and shower. She is an attorney for a division of the city called the Senior Citizen Advocate Bureau. Senior citizens in our city are able to obtain free legal advice and representation in court."

Rudy was obviously acquainted with the service. I can only imagine the stories Bulla and he made up to get the city attorneys on his side. The police told us it was legal for us to have the cameras.

"Thomas, don't shoot the messenger. I'm just telling you what Thelma told me to tell you: to take them down."

"Did you tell her that they were not pointed at their house, that they were just taping our house and driveway?"

"Thomas, that was your little project. I told Thelma to call you later at home to discuss it."

"How did they have your work telephone number? If it is a city matter they have no right bothering you at work, especially as it was connected to me and not you. When did she say she was going to call?"

"She did not say."

"Well, I am not going to take them down. That is our protection from those two whackos. Did you tell her the police told us it was okay?"

"Yes, I did. Thelma said the police did not know what they're talking about."

"Who should I believe?"

"Just leave them running. Let's see what happens."

Therefore, I left them up. They still were serving their purpose protecting our house and animals. Three days went by without Thelma calling me. Then on Friday evening around six, when I was sitting on the porch having a beer, two little white city cars pulled up in front of our house. Three young, tall, very strong men got out of one car and the other car produced a woman with bright red shoulder length hair that curled at the bottom. The curls must have had hairspray to hold them in place and they looked rather contrived. She was dressed in a light gray business suit. The men were dressed in jeans and T-shirts and looked as though they spent part of their week in the gym lifting weights. The woman looked a bit older. I would have guessed her to be in her forties. She was around five feet two inches tall and she looked fit and ready to fight. They looked into our porch, walking at a strong pace right for the front door.

I called to Barbara, "Barbara, we have company."

I stood up and got to my front door before they did.

"May I help you?"

"Is your name Thomas Smith?"

"Yes it is. What is the nature of your business with me?" as if I was unaware of the reason why they came over.

"May we come in?"

I looked at Barbara for her thoughts.

"Sure, let them in."

I figured this must be Thelma and three sidekicks to show muscle. The three men tried to intimidate by standing very close to my right, left, and back, while Thelma stood in front of me.

"Thomas, you need to take down the cameras."

I wanted her to realize why my living situation here was so bad that I needed to put up security cameras. So I decided to show them the mum stomper tape. Perhaps, once they had seen Rudy in action that would put them on our side. The VCR and television were on the porch from when the police came over. I left Barbara on the porch and went to retrieve the tape. When I returned the air was still void of any sound. None of them had even shifted their sitting positions. They looked like wax museum figures.

Before I put the tape in the VCR I explained to them that Officer Adamik had viewed the tape and wanted to arrest Rudy. I explained that I had told the officer I did not want to have him arrested right then. I did not want to tell her or the police about the other tapes I held. At that time I did not want to put all my cards on the table.

I had rewound the tape earlier so that if I had to show it again I would not have to waste time finding the beginning of the tape that showed him stomping our mums.

I pressed start on the remote so that they could watch the same scene that I had shown to Adamik. I had my response all ready for what I was sure they would say. Barbara and I were in for a shock.

Thelma was the first to speak. "That's nothing. It looks nothing like Rudy. That is no proof."

The three men chimed in, supporting Thelma's view. "I don't see anything on that tape."

We heard what they were saying, but believing what we were hearing was the difficult part. Their comments left us speechless.

Thelma said, "You will have to take them down. If not you will have to go to court."

She was an attorney and we guessed that the three men were doing some kind of dirty work for her. If they had a mind to, they could take us to court. We were saving for a house to buy. We could not afford a lengthy legal battle costing us thousands while Rudy was getting his attorney free. Thelma asked if I had permission from our property owner to put up the camera system. I looked at Barbara and she confirmed the fact that she had talked to him on the telephone.

Barbara said, "Yes, he laughed and told me it was a good idea."

They stood up and bid us a good night. The last thing Thelma said was, "Take those cameras down."

I did not take them down. I thought after I told her that the landlord said it was OK, it was a bit strange that the last thing she said was to take them down.

A week went by with no police and no lawyers. Then it came. I received a call from Thelma. She sounded angry. "I'm telling you to take down those cameras. I called the property owner and asked him if he gave you written permission before you put the cameras up. He said he did not give you written permission. According to the law you must have written permission from your landlord before putting up the cameras." The smart thing was to take them down to avoid court time and attorney fees. I told her I would take them down and then get written permission.

"Even if you do get his written permission you must not capture Rudy's property on your tape."

I agreed, telling her that I would take every precaution not to have their property show up in my taping as I already had been taping with that in mind.

I called Barbara at work and told her of my conversation with Thelma. We had to get written permission from the landlord to keep up the security system. She was quite concerned that he would get mad.

"Try to make him understand that if we do not have those cameras on Rudy could do serious damage to the house. Tell him he turned on the back faucet and the water could have caused quite a bit of damage to his house. Tell him he is escalating his attacks. This would be a real solution to him being a problem."

"Thomas, I know him. He will not want to get involved."

"Just ask him, please. If he will not give us the permission in writing I will try plan B."

"Oh Thomas, I'm afraid to ask. What is plan B?"

"Plan B is that I will just look as though I am taking down the cameras. In fact, I will make sure he sees me taking them down. I will wait two weeks and then put them back up. This time I will pick up some cameras with new technology, making them undetectable. I will be extremely careful as to hiding their presence as well as the installation. The police said it was okay."

"Rudy will bring those lawyer dogs on us if he catches you putting them up, which could be a lot of trouble. I don't like this. You are going to get us in trouble."

"Barbara, we are already in trouble."

Barbara called Fred but could not get him to answer his telephone. It just kept going to voicemail. After the fifth message she left he finally returned her call. He was not going to put his permission in writing.

"I finally got a return call from Fred."

"Who the heck is Fred?"

"Thomas, you just don't listen to me. Our landlord's name is Fred."

"We always just called him "the landlord.""

"I know, but his name is Fred."

"Did you explain to him that it was really in his best interest to let us put the cameras up?"

"I guess he thinks it will cause more trouble. Bulla and Rudy, and now the lawyers, have both his telephone numbers, here and in Florida. They will just call him every day until he throws us out."

"This is really something. The police are on our side, yet the city lawyers seem to be intent on obstructing justice. A strange paradox, wouldn't you say?"

Barbara used her favorite expression: "Indeed."

"What I cannot figure out is, why the city lawyers are all on the side of Bulla and Rudy. They viewed the same tape the police viewed, yet came away hating us, the good guys, in all of this."

"Thomas, you only think of the present. They have most likely been in contact with Thelma for years now, telling her their version of the facts on anything that took place in the prior weeks and years. Don't you think they were calling Thelma on Anna all that time?"

"Barbara, you know, Anna did retaliate on Bulla and Rudy. So they probably called the police and Thelma to document what Anna had done to them. If I know them, and I think do, they just sat on that porch and made up minor situations that led up to the crazy things Anna would do to them. When Thelma and those three men sat on our porch they seemed blinded to the truth. Thelma watched him stomping the mums. I think you could show her all the incriminating tapes we have on them and she still would come up with a similar reaction."

"Remember, they are truly evil with no care for what is right or wrong. Rudy said it best when he told you, this is how we get our jollies."

"They go to church every Sunday. What is up with that?"

"Thomas, you just do not think as they do. After church they have coffee and cookies with the other parishioners, discussing all the wrongs they suffered through the week."

"How do you know that?"

"Do you think I'm making this stuff up?"

"No, but how do you know?"

"I have lived on this street for a long time. People talk. People hear gossip and come up to me when I'm walking the dog to tell me what they heard. There are not too many secrets around here. They all are aware of what goes on. I had mentioned Thelma's name to our neighbor Judy who lives in the house behind us. Judy knows who Thelma is. She confirmed that Bulla talks to Thelma after church services."

"How come Thelma does not hear the other side of what is going on here?"

"People in our neighborhood just do not want to get involved. They are afraid of starting anything with the bullies. Who wants the police coming to their house week after week? They may go to church just to discuss their neighbor problems with Thelma. The fact is that Thelma is on their side against us. To her the truth does not matter."

I took down the cameras, making sure that Rudy and Bulla were outside so that they could see me removing them. I saw them gloating as I removed them. I was not going to just take them down and leave everything I owned at the mercy of those unbalanced ones. I searched the Internet for spy equipment and found a retail shop that specialized in that kind of stuff. I called and went out to the store to meet with the owner and explain my situation so that he could suggest cameras that would be undetectable. The equipment was quite expensive but I felt that it would be worth every penny.

This time the plan would be to cut the grass myself. I would put the mower in the shed and it should not take long before Bulla would find me cutting the grass with the gas mower unbearable. Then Rudy would sabotage the gas mower as he had done to Barbara before. I would have it on tape so that I could make a police report and have him arrested. This time, with so much evidence, the Judge would have to put him in jail. That footage, along with all the other footage I already had in our safety deposit box, would show malicious intent for bodily harm. This would be worth the wait.

Everything was peaceful or should I say quiet for about two weeks. I never could quit smiling when I got home and Rudy was working on his plants and shrubs from his side of the driveway. This was a big win and I could not help but rub it in. I would wave and smile hello when he looked up. He learned quickly not to look up when the car pulled in the driveway. In that case I would say in my happiest voice, "What a great day to do some gardening, wouldn't you say, Rudy?"

Maybe, heckling him was not the smartest thing to do. It just felt so good to have the upper hand after all that had happened: the faucet, hose, and the mums, the lawnmower blowing up, the most hateful comments over the fence, destroying the grass in the backyard, and the film of bringing their dog over every morning to pee on our lawn. It may have seemed like a small retaliation to the rest of the world but our hands were mostly tied with the city lawyers on their side. Under the circumstances it was a good start. I felt elated every time I pulled into the driveway.

It was not enough. I needed justice. The driveway restriction was like a drug: once tasted, the brain wanted more. He could not be sure that somewhere the cameras were not running. I had to make sure I put them up without being discovered. Not easy tasks when those two sets of eyes were always watching.

I found myself thinking of ways to get those creeps. I could feel myself being pulled down to their level; I had not crossed the line of legality yet, so I justified my actions to myself.

I would get permission from Fred to put up a fence between the properties. This would do two things. Stop them from constantly peeking out of their windows and make it impossible to work on those shrubs and flowers. It would affect the sunlight as well. I would have to first study city code to figure out how high could it be, how close to the property line, and what other restrictions there would be. I thought I could sell Fred on the wisdom of having the privacy of a fence, not only for us, but for anyone who would move in there after us. The house was old and I certainly did not want to buy it. The cost of the fence was an expenditure I could accept.

I called Fred but he refused. He said it would just cause him more problems with Bulla and Rudy and he could not take their constant calls. I tried to convince him that it would cause fewer problems for now and in the future. He did not buy my argument.

I was angered after I hung up the telephone. It really looked as though he was on their side. That had to be it. He was blaming us for not getting along with them. Fred did not understand. Even if we left and he got new tenants things would not change. There would just be different people living there and they would start to attack them. Perhaps Fred thought that since we never complained to him his only problem was us aggravating them. Barbara figured they complained all the time to Fred. She said Fred would not return their calls. He mentioned to Barbara that he knew they were nuts. Fred never spoke to us about the content of their calls. The rent came in steadily and that was all he worried about.

Fred not writing the letter of permission for the cameras and him not standing with us against them angered me. We paid him the rent every month on time, yet he did not want to take on any responsibility for being the property owner. I thought that unwillingness to stand up for us was wrong.

MASTER PLAN

Our landscapers came to cut the grass once a week. After they left Barbara and I were sitting outside on our backyard patio enjoying the summer breeze, when out came Bulla.

"What the hell! You tell your landscapers that they nearly blew out our window with either the mower or the blower. Rocks were hitting it. If it broke we would be killed by flying glass."

I said, "Bulla, Which one was it, the mower or the blower?"

"I don't give a damn. Flying rocks hit our window."

"Well, if it breaks let me know and I will get the landscapers to pay for it."

She was just making a big deal out of nothing. No way could a rock be thrown that distance to break her window. I did not say anything to her because they were impossible to reason with. All I could think of to say was, "I will get the landscaper to pay for it." That made her angry and I knew it would. She did her usual huff and puff and disappeared back into the house. The week went by fast and it was time for the landscapers to come cut the grass. First they did some work for a neighbor who lived three doors away from us. I looked out the window, knowing that they were coming and saw Rudy discussing something with Felipe. Felipe was not his landscaper, so I ran out of the house and to the truck. Before I reached the truck I yelled, "Hey, what do you think you're doing? What business do you have talking to my landscaper?"

His answer was, "So I cannot talk to your landscaper?"

"I said, "No. Talk to me if you have a problem and I will talk to Felipe."

He was far away from his property and he had nothing more to say. He looked slightly afraid for his safety. He just gave me a cold stare and walked away. I asked Felipe what Rudy had said to him. Felipe said nothing.

"Felipe, he was talking to you for two minutes. I saw his mouth moving. What did he say?"

"Thomas, he said the lawnmower throw rocks and hit his window. I don't want any trouble with him. I know him; he makes trouble for me."

"Okay Felipe, do not worry, I will take care of him."

Barbara thought that Felipe was also afraid of Rudy. He was probably afraid he would call the city to get him in trouble. This was just more bullying.

I was concerned for Felipe. He had a hard job and did not need this aggravation on top of his most difficult job. I didn't think I could protect him. I called him during the week. We talked and decided that it would be best for all if I cut the grass. I could tell that he was actually relieved at his dismissal.

Rudy gave me the opportunity to set a trap that I had been waiting for, one that could get him in serious trouble with the law. I would buy a gas-powered mower and cut the grass myself. I knew that when they saw me cutting the grass they would go nuts. Our driveway had weeds and rocks, so a few passes should do it. No rocks would hit their window but they would be infuriated merely at the fact that I was cutting the weeds in the driveway.

I put the gas mower in the unlocked shed, waiting for Bulla to demand Rudy to do something about that dangerous lawnmower. This time I had the new wireless cameras that would transmit images to my computer. I had two of them, one inside the shed and the other one focused outside the shed, in case he pulled it out to work on it. I would get that recorded as well. I knew he thought all the cameras were gone and would not suspect them because if he had seen any cameras, he would surely have called the city lawyers to come back and harass us again. So now the lawyers were doing us a favor by warning us that they were detected. I took great pains in disguising the placement of the cameras. Now all I had to do was just sit tight, waiting for the grass to grow.

Barbara's mood and mine were lifted by the setting of our latest trap. The first night she came home from work after I brought home the lawnmower she asked me if we had anything on tape. I snickered and politely said, "Honey, I have not cut the grass yet." I knew then how excited she was, partly because of him ruining two of her lawnmowers.

"Barbara, please be patient. He will bite but it is going to take several weeks. I need to cut the grass a few times to bring out their insanity and to get them to do something very foolish. As sure as bees are attracted to the sweet smell of flowers, he will find the temptation too great to avoid. He has done it twice before and has never even been questioned for it, so what is to stop him now?"

One nice sunny Sunday, I noticed some cars parked on our street. I did not recognize them and upon closer examination I noticed out of town plates.

"Hey, Barbara, looks like Bulla and Rudy are having some people over."

"Yes, a backyard barbeque. They probably were some distant relatives. They hadn't had anyone over for years."

"I have never seen anyone visit them."

"It happens just once every five or ten years."

I went out in the backyard to work on the lawnmower and Barbara watched me put the gas in so that she could learn how to operate it in case she had to cut the grass. One of Bulla's relatives recognized Barbara and asked Bulla, "Is that Daniel there with Barbara?"

"No, Daniel died five years ago."

"Sorry to hear that. Who is that, her new boyfriend?"

Bulla blurted out louder than necessary, just for us to hear. "Yes, that is Thomas, some bum she picked up in some bar."

That really was not nice and made me angry.

I looked at Barbara and said, "What the hell was that?"

"That was Bulla being Bulla."

"The weeds in the gravel driveway are getting long. Let's see how our new lawnmower works." I turned the key to the lawnmower. There was no explosion. The engine roared, spit a little, and then just had a smooth, strong running sound to the motor. I was relieved as I headed for the driveway. I noticed that their barbecue had food cooking on it.

I said to myself, "A bum she picked up in a bar! What would a bum do in a situation like this?"

I proceeded to cut the driveway. It had not rained for at least two weeks. Rocks and dust came up and the wind was blowing right toward their barbecue. I saw that Rudy had to quickly cover the grill to prevent the food from being covered with dust. I decided to show them how a bum cuts the weeds in the driveway. That drive-way needed several passes to ensure the grassy weeds were cut, short enough to suit our neighbors. Then, of course, there was the nice grass to cut. Overall, I took an hour to cut the grass, which could have been cut in fifteen minutes. I just kept going over it and eventually I drove them out of the backyard and into the house.

I felt bad for their visitors; my thinking and actions were a reaction to being called a bum to people that I didn't know. I was angry and wanted to get back at them. At the same time I felt it was an opportunity to infuriate them which should do a lot to hurry up the sabotage I was expecting to happen. The man was cautious and did not want to make it obvious, so I knew he would take his time to retaliate. I assumed he would cause no more problems until his attack but I kept the cameras rolling just in case. I did not want to miss anything. This would mean at least an assault charge if not assault, and then maybe attempted murder.

I wanted to win this one. We had done nothing wrong but made a few honest mistakes: we were always ready to make amends. They were unforgiving and perpetually on the attack, to the point that they didn't mind crossing the line of legality.

Every night when I got home from work, before I did anything, I watched those security tapes. The tapes showed nothing. Could I have missed something? If I missed something I could get blown up. A week went by and it was time to cut the grass. As a joke, I asked Barbara if she would start the lawnmower for me and told her I would be right out to cut the grass. She picked up on it right away.

"Thomas, this was your idea. I'm not having that thing explode in my face."

I laughed and went out to the shed. I pulled it out away from the house in case the damn thing caught on fire. I did not want to seem tentative as I never knew when they were watching. I gave it a quick turn of the key and was a bit startled when the engine turned over on the first turn. I went about cutting the lawn and those nasty weeds in the driveway with all those rocks. I thought for sure that they would come out swinging but they didn't. That showed me it was very possible that they had something much more sinister planed.

I took my time doing the lawn work, making as much noise and dust as humanly possible. Gosh, this was crazy fun. I remember Rudy saying when I asked him why he was doing all those horrible things to us, "This is how we get our jollies."

I was enjoying this too much, perhaps, but there was no turning back now. The wind had broken off one of their flowers and they blamed us for snapping it. The flower was adjacent to where Barbara parked her car, so they assumed she did it. That was the rationale for eight months of retaliation.

There was no telling what he would put in that tank next time. I watched intently every day. The cameras still could get good images without a light on in the shed. I did not want to do anything to scare him off. We were home at night; we did not think he would risk himself going in at night. I could not be sure, so I put a small piece of clear tape on the gas tank cap. If the clear tape was not broken, no one tampered with it. If it were broken, I would know it had been unscrewed.

The next week was again nerve-racking due to the fact that I had to cut the grass again. I did not see anything on the cameras but one never knows what could happen when you are up against such a deviate. I pulled out the gas mower and looked in the gas tank to check the level. It was a low due to the one-hour running the week before, so I filled the tank and tightened the gas cap. As I was filling the tank it occurred to me that he could have tampered with the can that I kept the extra gas in. Could he have put something there, knowing that I would have to fill up the tank? Was that on the video I was watching? I grabbed the key in between my finger and thumb, held my breath, and turned it to the on position. It did not start like the first time. I had to think for a minute. Should I try it again? Did I miss seeing something on the tapes? Did he sneak in the shed at night to do his dirty work? The tape was intact and not broken but doubt was creeping in. Would I have third degree burns over fifty per cent of my body?

My brain said, "Turn it on, chicken."

I did and it started. I began breathing again. Now I would just cut the grass normally in a normal period. I would not go near the rocks in the driveway. No dust flying in the air, a shorter cut time. Rudy would think I had forgotten or I was thinking he was not going to retaliate for the dust storm I created at his barbecue. I knew better; he would never forget. He would try to get back at me tenfold. I just needed to make sure the cameras were transmitting. I had to keep those tapes rolling.

For another week I did not see them every day, which was curious. Then two weeks later, on a Wednesday night, I came home and like every other night, the first thing I would do was go to my control center and view the tapes.

What a Wednesday it was! I watched that grey-haired monster sneaking into the shed to put something in the tank.

Barbara came home while I was watching the tape for the twentieth time.

"Honey, come downstairs. We've got him good this time."

"What did you get?"

"I got Rudy putting something in our gas tank."

"Oh my! Let me see."

I rewound the tape to just before he opened the shed door and entered with a bottle of something in his hand. The tape showed him unscrewing the gas cap and pouring something in the mower tank.

"That crazy fool! Is he trying to kill us? What are you going to do with this tape?"

"I will call Officer Adamik in the morning and tell him what happened here."

"Are you going to have Rudy arrested?"

"Have to wait until I talk to him, to see if we have all that we need to put him away. I don't want him to be hit by a ruler on his hands for being a bad boy. I want time."

"The officer is really going to want to arrest Rudy."

"Yes, he will but it is my decision. Remember last time he said we had time to have him arrested. I'm going to ask Officer Adamik to test the gasoline to see if it could be lethal or just some sugar that would ruin the engine. You see, according to the law they are two different offenses. If it turns out that he used something that could cause bodily harm, he can kiss his ass goodbye. I could not make out on the tape if he had gloves on or not. They might be able to pull a print off the gas cap. I am not going to touch a thing until Officer Adamik comes over and watches the tape. Then we will go out and he can call the lab to have the engine tested or whatever they do. I'm guessing that is how it will go down. Just do not touch anything out there."

"Thomas, sometimes you say some crazy things like I must not go anywhere near that thing."

"I know I'm just nervous. I don't want anything to happen to the evidence."

"Just chill out for now. Have a few beers with me and we will sleep well tonight and deal with it all tomorrow."

"I will not go to work. I will call the police and see what they want to do or what time they can come over."

"Good. Just keep me updated on what is happening."

"No problem."

I really did not sleep well, even with the beer. I waited until 9:00 am to see if I could get hold of Officer Adamik. He was not in and the operator took a message for him to call me.

She asked me if it was an emergency. I answered. "I believe a crime was committed and I do not want the crime scene to become contaminated, so in that respect, yes, it is an emergency."

She said, "I will page him for you now."

I got a call back in thirty minutes.

"Hello. Thomas speaking."

"Hello. Thomas Smith?"

"Yes, this is me."

"This is Officer Adamik. What's up?"

"I have another videotape I think you will want to see."

"I need more information Thomas."

"Okay, sorry. I have a tape of Rudy putting something in the gas tank of my lawnmower. I am afraid to start it because it may blow up."

"Are you home now?"

"Yes."

"I will be there in ten minutes. Do not touch anything."

"I will see you there."

The squad car pulled in the driveway and I ran to the back door to let him in.

"Hi, officer. Would you please follow me? I saw Rudy do something in the gas tank of the power mower. Come in the back door. The tapes are downstairs now."

"Did you touch anything after you saw him in there?"

"No sir."

I played the tape for him. He only had to see it once. Immediately he made a call to the station. I did not make out what he was asking for exactly but I assumed he called the technician for fingerprints and evidence gathering.

He got up and asked to be shown the shed where the lawnmower was. We left through the back door and I showed him the shed."

"He said, "Do not touch anything."

I said, "No problem."

Then he excused himself and went to the squad car to make another telephone call and started his paperwork. I just went back into the house to wait for instruction. I had questions for him. I thought the tape was plenty but if he had put anything lethal in the tank it would be a much bigger deal. Along with the other tapes I could have him put away and silence Bulla forever. Of course, after the legal suit there would be the civil suit. This is why I did not ever want to do anything illegal. We were very safe in those regards. Justice would be our revenge.

I knew Rudy and Bulla were watching all this. They were probably going nuts over there. They would be on "pins and needles" until the police left or went to them for questioning. I was sure they did not know about the cameras because they would have called Thelma and would have never gone into the shed to sabotage the gas tank in the lawnmower.

When I first moved in I tried to be a good neighbor but things changed. It seemed that just to stay sane I had to fight every day. There was no way to quit when the other people just kept attacking us where we lived. I felt like a punching bag for a sadist to punch whenever he wanted to make himself feel good. This was definitely sociopathic behavior.

This had now been going on since I moved in and my dear wife Barbara had been enduring these living conditions for many years. We had developed many symptoms that a bullied child has in school. Barbara and I were not bullied in school. In fact, we both had nice personalities and were liked by almost all. We both were determined not to bow down to this ridiculous aggression without fighting them with all our mental ability. When we were young and ventured out into the working world, we had another thing in common: If we felt that, our boss was unappreciative or abused us at our jobs we would just walk out the door. Both of us left two jobs for the same reason. Our situation was different here. This was where we lived and some basic instinct kicked in. That instinct was to protect the possessions: property, animals, loved ones, and the wellbeing of the place where we lived. Barbara felt, just as Anna did, that for her own dignity's sake she would not bow to the bullies.

Thirty minutes after the officer went to his car another squad car pulled up. Two officers came out, one woman and a man. The woman had a shoulder bag with her. The detective directed them to the shed. He explained what I had told them, so they dusted for prints and took a sample of the gas. I ran out the back door. Officer Adamik said I should wait inside and he would get me when they were done. A little later I heard him knock at the front door.

"Come on in. Where do we go from here?"

He came in and sat on our porch.

"Mr. Smith, when they report the lab results to me I will call you right away. I believe I have your telephone numbers here. Are these your numbers where I can reach you?"

He showed me his lengthy report. I answered yes. "I need to ask you a couple of questions."

"Sure Thomas. Go ahead."

"I had not mentioned this before because honestly, I was very confused. Ever since I put up the first cameras they have been calling you complaining. One of your officers came out and told them it was legal for us to do so. A couple of days after the first officer came to us to explain their complaint, a lawyer from the Senior Citizen's Advocate Bureau of the city called Barbara at work. She was very harsh with her and demanded we take down the cameras. She explained that we need those cameras to protect our home from those two. Barbara even asked her if she wanted to see the tape of him stomping our mums. Well, she came over here with three young men dressed in denim and T-shirts. I showed the tape you saw of him stomping the mums. They said the tape showed nothing and was worthless. Then she demanded we remove the cameras."

The officer just shook his head. His lips tightened as to hold back on saying something he should not.

"I left the cameras up. Rudy noticed immediately and had that lawyer call me again. This time she stated that we needed approval from our landlord. I told her Barbara had called our landlord and he not only said it was okay, but he also told us it was a good idea. She then hung up and two days later called again to say we needed written permission from him to have the cameras up. She threatened to have us in court for the rest of our lives if I did not comply. We are saving to buy a house and we could not afford being pulled into court to defend ourselves from their false accusations. That lawyer called our property owner and bullied him. He then said he gave us verbal permission but he did not want to get involved with giving us written permission. He just did not want to get involved on that level. I talked to my lawyer and he assured me of my right as a renter that as long as I did not cause damage to his property it was legal on my part to put up security cameras, especially since I had that tape of prior damage. I went out and bought much more expensive cameras that were undetectable. This is why he was confident not to get caught. He thought it a simple operation to come into the shed to sabotage the lawnmower. If he knew I had the cameras he never would have attacked us. The city attorney would have called and threatened us to take them down as she had done before."

"Let's see what is in your lawnmower. I could arrest him now, if you wish."

"I would enjoy that but I want to wait to see what he put in there. If it was just something to ruin the lawnmower I know the punishment will not fit the crime. He will get off way too easy. I don't think anyone could understand the terror we feel everyday living here."

"Mr. Smith, do not retaliate in such a manner that you break the law yourself."

"No sir, I am just not like that. I am thinking about a civil suit. If he loses money, he will then realize his actions against others will have serious consequences. You told me before I do not have to act immediately on having him arrested. Is that correct?"

"Yes, Mr. Smith. I will call you as soon as the lab reports are in."

"Thank you officer, I will be waiting for your call."

Barbara and I were nervous the next day, waiting for the information. When no call came I asked Barbara, "Should I call Officer Adamik?"

"No. He will call you when they know something."

My imagination was very active. I was daydreaming a court scene where I showed tape after tape until the final one where he put the lethal liquid in the mower's tank. When the jury foreman was asked to read the verdict, guilty on all counts, Barbara and I started to cry. As I came out of my daydream, a squad car pulled up in front of our house.

"Barbara, come here. Adamik is here."

There were two police officers in the squad car. Only Adamik came to the house. He had a briefcase with him. I opened the door and held it for him to enter.

As he walked through the door I blurted out; "Was it an explosive?"

"Take it easy, Thomas. Sit down, and we will go over the results."

My heart was pounding and I am sure Barbara's blood pressure was sky-high.

Officer Adamik said, "The lab found sugar in the gasoline. It would ruin the motor but not cause the mower to explode."

He looked to us as both of our heads dropped in disappointment. Yes, we had him on yet another minor charge of destruction of property. With no other arrest and the Judge considering his age and income, which was just Social Security, the law might not take into account all the hours, days, weeks, months, and years of being unjustly terrorized by those two people, who caused us emotional stress for years, "just to get their jollies."

Officer Adamik said, "Would you like me to arrest him now?"

"Yes, please do."

The officer stood up and asked me for all the evidence I had. He started to leave to arrest Rudy and I followed him with my camera to take a short movie of this memorable occasion. He stopped just outside our door and turned to face me. "Thomas, I'm going to ask you to stay in your house. Do you understand me?"

"Yes," I said, "but the moment of arrest would make for a great movie."

"For now, just stay in the house. You will be informed of any further actions."

I went back in and Barbara asked me what was going on. I told her he just told me to go back in the house and they would contact us. We watched from the front porch as they brought him out in handcuffs. Walked him to the back seat of the police car, held one hand on his head and delivered him to the back seat of the squad car.

The next day I was called in to sign complaint forms. Rudy was back home after posting bail. Officer Adamik told us his court date would be in about three months. I asked him if I was going to have to appear and he said no. I asked him for the date because I wanted to be at his trial. He said he would get back to me with a date and time.

OVER THE EDGE

I called my lawyer friend Steve the next day to see what he thought about a civil action. Steve had several other attorneys working with him in his firm. I would not ask him as just a favor. That would be unprofessional. With the idea of a civil suit Steve and his firm could make some money if they took the case on consignment. With all the evidence I had, they thought they could win. My thinking was if they faced a real threat to lose a considerable amount of money they would stop terrorizing us. At the least, the police now had plenty of information on them. Their rants would be considered questionable and unsubstantiated, while our complaints would be documented.

They knew what they had done and had seen the police come to our house. What they did not know is the amount of tape we had on them. I was quite tickled by this event. Barbara, on the other hand, began to worry.

"What about their city lawyer? Will our videotape stand up in court? She said we needed written permission to put up the cameras."

"I told you that their attorney was bluffing about written consent by the landlord. He did give us verbal consent. We know Fred well enough that he would not lie under oath. We have our rights as tenants. Their attorney bluffed Fred and us into believing that he had to give us written permission. We would need legal permission to, let us say, move a wall. We have every right to take movies wherever we want as long as we are not pointing the cameras in their windows. Are you saying we cannot take pictures outside? See, that does not make sense. That is why the police kept telling us that we were not breaking the law by protecting ourselves with the cameras as long as the cameras were not filming any part of their house. I made sure from the very start that they were not."

We did not think to do something so underhanded, so we could not recognize that a city official could actually lie to us to get us to do what she wanted. We had thought she had by moral code of ethics to be honest. We both felt naive and betrayed by the system. If it ever happened, again we would handle it much differently. We would tell her to put it in writing. If she had put something in writing we could complain to that attorney's superior that she was harassing Fred with manipulative deceitful telephone calls.

We knew Rudy and Bulla would be looking for the cameras but the equipment I had bought was unbeatable. You could be looking directly at the camera and not know it was there. They would be very careful for now. As a last resort there was always a civil suit. I just needed some time to see exactly what was needed for a civil suit to stick. Maybe the actions had gone so far that they would stop them from messing with us.

"Thomas, you just don't get it, after all the time you've spent here. They are not normal. They will just sit around all day with nothing else to do except for coming up with things to destroy our peace and tranquility."

"I really think this time we have stopped them. The criminal court date is in three months. If we win there we can always take it to civil court were the stakes would be much greater, first things first, ok? Let us see what happens, this Judge could dish out a penalty and a warning that would keep them at bay."

THE CRIMINAL TRIAL

L ike a child waiting for Christmas, waiting for that day, the day that court would convene took forever. Even though the officer suggested we not be there, we knew we had the right to attend. After being helpless for so long, we believed it would be healing for our mental state to be there. The date was 9:00 a.m. the first Wednesday in October. We both had that day marked on our calendar. We arranged taking the whole day off, to attend the court date. We got to the courtroom thirty minutes early but the room had not opened yet. We leaned against the wall waiting for them to open the room. We wanted the first row, closest to the Judge.

"Barbara, this may get a little uncomfortable if Rudy and Bulla are also early and all of us are in the hall."

"Just stand there and stare at them as they have done to you for the last four years."

At first, I thought that Barbara exaggerated saying that they had been staring for all of the four years I had been living there. After thinking about it for a minute, I realized that she was not exaggerating. When they looked our way, it always was a look that they held for a longer time than normal people would display in an outside social neighbor situation. It made me uncomfortable and we were sure that was their intent. The best way to describe it is when, if a teacher was mad at you, having a look of pain on their face and refusing to look away, even if you looked away and looked back, they were still staring at you with a scowl.

We were not the only ones waiting for the courtroom to open. I had wondered if this was a criminal court or traffic court. It had the feeling of being very similar to traffic court. Traffic court punishment would be a joke. I said nothing to Barbara, as I was not sure of what the outcome would be. A clerk opened the door. I looked at my watch it was 8:45 a.m. I went in first and Barbara followed closely behind, sitting in the closest seats to the Judge , wanting to hear every word. Every time someone came into the courtroom, we turned our heads to see if they had arrived. I quit after a while as I was actually getting a pain in my neck from turning around.

We had been prepared mentally for a continuance. They arrived with the city attorney at 9:05 a.m. Barbara saw them enter the courtroom first. She tapped my leg.

I turned around to look at the three of them. Of course, Rudy and Bulla just stared at us as we stared back. The three of them also came to the front of the courtroom sitting just opposite us. They were truly professionals at making us uncomfortable. I did not see a video player in the courtroom. I then presumed the Judge had seen the tapes earlier.

I noticed that when the Judge came into the court-room it look very much like traffic court and after the first few cases were called we were assured of that being the case. Their case was the fifth one of the day called. The Judge asked them to confirm their names and they did. Then he read the grievances. One complaint against Rudy "stomping of the mums" and one against Bulla "intentionally bringing her dog to pee on our front lawn, in the exact spot twice a day." The court clerk asked them how they pled, they answered guilty. The Judge fined them $100.00 each and granted us $75.00 for damage to our personal property. Then he said something about everyone getting along and that he did not want to see him or her again.

I stood up in anger, as did Barbara. I almost shouted out something, but the sentence was so light I had nothing prepared for this outcome. We both just stood there in disbelief at what just occurred. All three of them paraded past us, just standing there watching them leave the courtroom. Bulla and Rudy looked at us as they passed with a smirk on their faces. Barbara and I said nothing, as we actually hadn't had time to process what just took place. We just walked out after them. They were ahead of us by about twenty paces.

Bulla blurted out, loud enough so we could hear, "Rudy did you see their faces as we walked by them out of the courtroom?"

We just stayed silent, still not knowing how to deal with everything at this point. I asked Barbara if she wanted breakfast and she agreed. We did not speak until we sat down at the restaurant.

I spoke first: "I don't know about you, I am really disappointed at the outcome of that. After all we put into it."

"Well Thomas, we have what they did documented and the Judge did tell them that any further aggressive actions from them would have serious repercussions."

"I would think so, however this might embolden them. You know how completely unpredictable they are."

"Thomas yes I do and I'm sure he will be waiting for me and you when we get home from work, every day to stare us down."

"This court trial could be a real good thing after all. They have officially pled guilty to the charged. Now we could sue them in a civil court for some real money and have fewer problems getting the cameras videos admitted as evidence."

"If you are going to go that way just make sure of the legalities and costs. Thomas we have done enough for now. I really think they will leave us alone."

"Maybe, but it's always good to have the civil court threat as an ace in the hole."

"Yes, indeed."

GOODBYE GOOD GIRL

Barbara's chocolate Labrador retriever became ill. The first thing we thought of was that the dog was poisoned. We rushed her to the vet and expressed our concerns. The vet came back with a diagnosis that the dog had a brain tumor, and was not poisoned. If they had poisoned our dog, only God knows what could have happened. Probably Barbara and I would be in jail.

Barbara was insistent on getting a puppy before winter and I could not say no. The puppy coming into our lives was important, as to what would happen next, regarding our relationship with the neighbors. She searched intently every day online until she found the right breeder for us to go look at the litter. I asked her to wait until spring so that the dog would be easier to train. She was heartbroken for her loss and I knew a puppy would really help. I did not agree to buy one but I did agree to go look, hoping that somehow I could convince her to wait until spring. We set up an appointment for Sunday, at one in the afternoon.

"Where is the breeder located?

"Not that far of a drive, just down south and a bit west."

She said it was Flanagan, Illinois. I had never heard of that town, so I came out with, "Is that about one and a half hours' traveling time?"

"Sure. It is not that far. Let's leave early, in case we get lost."

I had thought she was just anxious to get there. After two and a half hours, we were still on the interstate highway.

I said, "Aren't we there yet?"

"Almost, should be just up ahead."

We were in farmland. The corn was high. I did not see another car pass us for fifteen minutes and my imagination started to go wild. All those movies about being lost in the cornfield, with no way to get out came into play. Then the crazies really started to work on my mind. What if, this farm was owned by an escaped mental patient and the whole puppy thing was just a setup to lure us out into the farmland never to be heard from again? Our identities could be stolen and no one would ever find us. We could be looking at months of torture and a slow, painful death.

I was fine in the most dangerous parts of the city, yet the cornfields were throwing a fright into me. I confessed my worries to Barbara and she just laughed. She remembered one time we were lost in some small city on a dark street when some person crossed the street and came right up to us, asking for a light for his cigarette. Barbara was very nervous; she stood directly behind me, trying to avoid the first attack. I knew we were not in any danger. Later when we talked about it she asked how I knew we were not in danger. I told her that growing up in the city, one develops a certain instinct for such a thing. She wanted a better explanation. I said it was simple: two of us to one of them. Eighty per cent of the time you are outnumbered when attacked. She asked about the other twenty per cent and I explained she must not show any fear. Like an animal, one can sense it. I got a look from Barbara that said, "Who is this man?"

She held the map and asked to turn right at the next street and it should be on the left. I made up my mind right then to get a GPS. We found the farm. It looked nice and the driveway was clean. Most of my fears had vanished and I was as excited to see the litter as she was. We parked the car and began to walk up to the farmhouse. As we walked around the garage, we saw the owner on a blanket with the litter. Five puppies had different colored ribbons around their necks. The breeder had put the different colored ribbons on them so that we could tell them apart. I knew then that we were not leaving without one of them.

They were all solid medium brown with bright blue eyes. As this breed matured, their eyes turned brown. I had never owned this breed of dog, so I intended to leave the picking of the puppy up to Barbara. She had experience with picking out a puppy, so I trusted her to pick out the right one. Barbara sat on the corner of the blanket with the breeder. I stood about ten feet from them. Barbara was watching the litter for personality traits. She did not want the one that looked to be a couch potato. Nor did she want one with aggressive behavior traits. We were making small talk with the breeder when one of the puppies broke out of the pack. The puppy with the blue ribbon walked directly over to me and rested her body on my shoe. That was it for me; I fell in love.

Barbara did not make her decision on that. I of course hoped and prayed that she would pick the one that picked me, the one with the blue ribbon. She really took her time talking to the breeder and watching all five puppies for behavior traits. She questioned the breeder on what she had known of the puppies' personalities. I could not take it any more after twenty minutes and I walked back to the car to have a comfortable seat. After ten minutes I left the car and approached the two women and the five little ones.

"Well, Barbara, have you decided which one will be going home with us?"

My heart was pounding but I left the decision up to her. I was already in love with the one who had picked me. She gave them all a final look and picked the one with the blue ribbon. The three of us had a long drive home. The corn still made me uncomfortable and I was glad when we drove up to the highway, back to civilization. I knew these thoughts were silly, so I did not express my feelings to Barbara. She had noticed my body language and said, "Feel better now?"

We both started to laugh. I meekly said, "Yes, I do," which in turn brought on another round of laughter.

DON'T JUMP ON ME

W e experienced no trouble from Bulla and Rudy. We did not talk to them nor they to us. Oh, don't get me wrong they still took every advantage to stare us down every chance they had. The winter was coming, it was predicted to be a snowy, cold winter so their time would be limited for outside exposure. I could not imagine anything happening, yet they continued to surprise us.

Fall turned into winter. Anyone who has raised a large dog puppy knows of the work involved. We blended our knowledge of training a puppy to maturity – a period of one to three years – and started the most difficult the first year of training. This period is so important to either having a good dog or one that is out of control. Like new parents of a human child, we did not totally agree on how to raise our new baby. We were a compatible couple and the puppy was a test of and now a testimonial to that fact because of our give-and-take of training techniques. She let me do most of the disciplining; she was, in my opinion, too soft with a dog that was going to be seventy pounds of muscle.

We could see the puppy growing. On a weekly basis, one of us would comment on how she had grown. Barbara did not want a couch potato; she had picked one with some spunk compared to the others in the litter. Well, it turned out she had a little too much spunk and wanted to be the leader of her new pack. I had to show her that I was the leader of the pack, which was not easy since she had much more spirit and energy than we first had thought.

Walking on a leash was becoming more and more challenging as she grew stronger with every passing day. She loved all people and would jump on them with her two front paws to say hello when first meeting with them. Bou-Bou did not know her own strength and her paws had protruding nails that would scratch when she jumped up to greet you. We cut them as often as possible, yet the breed just has those kind of nails. Bou-Bou always wanted to take the lead. She meant no harm. She was just a happy puppy who loved people.

Barbara would give her dogs the lead, which might have been okay with a dog with less spirit. This dog would get so strong that she would eventually be able to pull Barbara and me off our feet on the icy sidewalks and streets, risking bodily harm.

We sat down over dinner to discuss the exact procedure we would use when we would take her out for her daily walks. We both had to be consistent with our instructions so as not to confuse or give her different signals. If we both were coordinated, the animal would learn much quicker. Time was important; Bou-Bou was growing and putting on weight and muscle every day. I brought out a paper and pencil and put a title heading on the page: "Walking Bou-Bou."

First, we would keep her on the sidewalk until we decided she could go on the grass. While on the sidewalk, if she insisted on pulling we would stop and tell her to sit. If she did not comply we would just stay there until she did. A short leash is most important to keep control during the training period.

When she walked on the cement sidewalks without pulling we would let the leash go slack. As soon as she took out the slack we would give the leash a tug and use the verbal command, "No." We would then stop moving forward and tell her to sit and then we would sit for a minute.

Time flew by and the first snowfall was a big one. I asked Barbara not to walk Bou-Bou in front of Bulla and Rudy's house. I just wanted to stay away from those freaks. I could not imagine anything happening but I did not want to take any risk with them. To be on the safe side, I asked her not to walk in front of them.

She answered, "I'm not going to let them dictate where I can walk and where I can't walk."

I said to myself, "Oh boy, this is not good."

Every night after she came home from work she would take Bou-Bou out and walk in front of their house, on the city sidewalk. Another eight inches of snow had fallen and from shoveling, the sidewalk had built up to three to four feet of snow, so there was no grass or sidewalk for Bou-Bou to go on. She elected to pee in the driveways where the snow had been removed, not just Bulla and Rudy's but whenever the urge hit her. We would pick up the solids and the other water would freeze or wash away with the melting snow. I asked Barbara to pull her in, if she was going to elect to pee in Rudy's driveway, just to keep the peace.

I asked Barbara again to walk her to the left, away from the front of Rudy and Bulla's house. I had Rudy pretty well stopped from attacking the house. He could not be sure if I had the cameras rolling or not.

I had my coat on to shovel some show off the front of the house while she walked the dog. She turned right and walked in front of their house. He was not outside, she turned right to walk right in front of their house on the public sidewalk. I just shook my head, I just asked her not to do that yet she was not going to cave into them and let them dictate her behavior. Sure enough Bou Bou picked Rudy's driveway to pee on and Barbara did not stop her.

Rudy must have been watching because as soon as she walked by their house he came out with his broom and took a stance in the middle of the sidewalk. He stood blocking Barbara from using it to return to our house. Snow on either side of the sidewalk prevented her from walking around him. She knew, in such close quarters, it would be impossible to pass him without the dog jumping on him. Even if the dog was just being playful, he might hit the dog with his broom or call the police and say he was attacked, even if it was a puppy.

I shouted to Rudy, "Just let her by."

He just stood there, legs spread apart, broom held across his body as if it was a rifle. I had stopped him on most fronts, yet he had found yet another way to intimidate us. Barbara had a problem with the ice and handling the dog. She and I were afraid that she could easily fall and hurt herself on the street.

He shouted out to her, "Keep that dog away from me."

"It is only a puppy, let me pass."

Barbara picked up the puppy and continued to walk towards him to one side. He held his broom very tight. She tried to push the broom out of her way, he was strong and would not let her by. He did not know that I was witness to this madness. The shovel I had in my hand was not a snow shovel but more of a spade. He would not let her pass on that public sidewalk, He had actually physically blocked her advance. I shouted out to her, "Just walk around on the street."

"No. I'm afraid I will fall on the ice."

"Rudy, for God sake let her by."

He would not move; he just stood there with that broom held tightly in his hands and she just stood there to face him down. She tried twice to push her way past, he held the broom firm prohibiting her advancement. Now he had threatened my wife and puppy and I just lost it. All those things I had been stuffing down for years started to bubble over. I lost my temper and I headed with shovel in hand to clear the walkway of that trash. Barbara saw me coming with shovel held shoulder-high, as if it was a baseball bat waiting to hit a homerun. Rudy's attention was on Barbara and the dog. I was coming up behind him going to swing.

The neighbor who lived to the left of me was out shoveling and was watching this drama play out.

He hollered out to me, "No, Thomas, no! It is not worth it."

Barbara also saw that this was going to get ugly fast, I saw her look over his shoulder to watch my advance with the shovel. She then backed off to walk around. It was close but I managed to gain control of my temper, which brought me back to some sort of reasonable thinking, although I was still fighting mad. On the way back to our home, I hit the steel banister with the shovel as hard as I could to let some of the pent-up emotion out. The vibration of the handle hurt my hands and the clang sound of the metal spade hitting the banister echoed like the bell of reapers' warning. My neighbor on the left, not sure what he had seen asked me:

"What the hell just happened there?"

"Rudy prevented her from using the sidewalk to return to our house by blocking the sidewalk with his broom"?

"Why did he do that?"

"Why? because he is insane."

I came into the house and Barbara and Bou-Bou came in a minute later. She unleashed Bou-Bou and started to curse. She was still quite wound up and so was I, but we did not discuss the incident.

I felt saying something like; "I told you so" but in this case that would do nothing for our relationship. Barbara knew that walking in front of his house might provoke him but she did not want to have him restrict her freedom of walking down a city sidewalk. I had a feeling something would happen someday but I did not expect things to go so wrong, so quickly.

Predicting his next move was very difficult. I said that I would call Officer Adamik in the morning and nothing more was said. It was a cowardly thing for Rudy to do, underhanded and despicable, but seeing that nothing happened, according to the law, there was nothing to do. He knew better than to strike her, as it would leave a mark. I should of just never have left the house without my camera, but this time I hadn't had my camera or my iPhone. No one would believe someone could act the way those two acted. Hell, my friends always thought I was exaggerating my stories, and indeed, I had toned some of them down just to make them more believable. Rudy did not know how close he came to having a lights-out moment.

I did not call the police the next day. I knew there was nothing the police could do. There are no laws about being a jerk and provoking an incident. We could stay here and continue this insanity until someone got hurt or just move out. The last incident was so close to someone getting hurt. I knew Barbara did not want to move but maybe she would look at it in a different light now that real danger was present. She saw me and the shovel coming at Rudy and knew that look I had in my eyes. She finally agreed to walk the dog to the left and not in front of their house. I could see this was a huge concession on her behalf and wondered if would hold. For her moving to another house, now more ever that was out of the question.

After the sidewalk incident Rudy had started up his creepy practice of making sure he was standing right on the property line with shovel or broom held diagonally across his chest as if it were a rifle. He would stare at me from the time I pulled in the driveway until I went into the house. OK, one may say so what, but let me tell you, day after day, week after week this was threatening. He did the same to Barbara. Her arrival time was more predictable, so he had missed a few days with me but Barbara would see him almost every single day. The action was unorthodox but effective. I was seriously a bit frightened as to what he would do next. Will he eventually crack and pull out a gun and shoot me dead in the driveway? I told myself that I was just letting my imagination run wild, and that is what he wanted. To cause me as much mental anguish as possible. I must just ignore him and some days I did. Yet every day, those cold crazy looking eyes and the face that never smiled were there, day after day.

HELPLESS?

I asked Barbara to move and rent another place again. Her answer came quickly, it was no. She had been there so long and the rent was cheap. We were saving for a nice house and it would not be long now. I could see her point, moving is difficult and to move and just move again in less than a year would be a hardship. She, like Anna, did not want to feel that, Bulla and Rudy had run her off, being stupidly justified in all the rotten things they had done to both our families. Just one more year and we should have the money needed to acquire a nicer house, in a better neighbourhood with hopefully friendly neighbours, and with our huge down payment our mortgage payment would be half of what we were paying for rent now. This is what we had been dreaming of.

I started to reflect on myself going forward. I was not the same man who moved four few years ago. I found myself thinking of more extreme ways to stand up for ourselves or was it just turning into revenge? Perhaps Rudy and Bulla developed their personalities from fighting with their other neighbours year after year? One huge problem is they would not let you quit the game. Even if we did nothing, said nothing, for six months, their attacks would continue. They assumed us helpless and they could just mess with us as they pleased. When we both were at work we were vulnerable. It seemed as if they thought of nothing else, since they could always surprise us with their latest attack. With him constantly attacking my family, something inside me was changing. I had not noticed it since it occurred at an unnoticeable pace. I had suppressed so much down inside. Like a ball you submerged in water the further you push it down the more pressure builds until one day you can't hold it down any longer and the ball slips out of your grip and create a huge disturbance. Now I was not only worried about him going off the deep end, I worried I might as well. I just wanted to live in peace, hell we did not have to love each other, not even say hello. We just wanted them to leave us alone. They would wait sometimes two months, making us think that everything was forgotten and we could live in peace and then for seemingly no reason they would come up with something new to infuriate us. I had definitely changed, spending more and more time thinking of ways to protect us. I was sinking more to their level, not acting out aggressively as they. However, by tracking my own thinking patterns I had been on that path for some time now. Thinking precludes actions, eventually a crazy idea, becomes a justified idea and starts to sound like a good idea. For a moment I lent this concept to excuse Bulla and Rudy's behaviour. Just for a moment, deep down inside, I did not want to think that poorly of humanity, the facts demonstrated to me that they just had to be evil.

JUST A MATTER OF TIME

Now our time left in that house was less than a year, not an eternity. I believed it was possible to finish our time in that house without a catastrophe. They had been to court, been warned by the Judge. All that did was redirect their efforts and make them more careful. We had the no trespassing restriction on them. I still had the cameras up and running. The cameras were not positioned for the sidewalk incident. I decided to move one of them to cover that. They rarely tried the same trick twice, but just maybe. Mostly, every day he would wait for me to come home to stare at me, big whoopee. Seeing my home arrival varied from one day to the next, I commended him on his fortitude as to spend some times as long as two hours waiting for my arrival home. With the end in sight, I told myself that

I would try hard not to do anything to aggravate them. Being blamed for Mother Nature was another thing all together, they would call the police to our house, we would answer the complaint and the police would leave. Whenever Barbara or I would go outside to do any maintenance around the house they would come out of their house to stand on their property line and just watch our every move, while remaining silent.

"Barbara, they must take turns just standing guard for us to come outside to try to intimidate us when we are out. Every time we go out if they are not out already they come out."

"Yeah, it gets to you after a while, they just always looked for anything we might do to use as an excuse to call the police."

By this time I threw my hands up and just quit trying, (for the ninetieth time). I needed to stop suppressing all this anger and needed an outlet to stay in control. I decided to have some fun with them. I would refuse to take them seriously any longer. They were going to remain silent, they could not step on our property, when I pulled my car into the driveway, one of them would be there. Most of the time now standing by the driveway to intimidate us was Rudy's responsibility. It was only the neighbourly thing to do was for me to say hello! I would roll down my window as I got close, I would stick my arm out the window and give him the finger while smiling. I wanted this to be entertaining, so each day along with the same gesture, with the intent of it not getting boring, I would come up with a different state-ment. A few examples are as follow:

"Hi Rudy, have you hit any puppies or small girls today, big man?"

"So glad you are watching our house for us today."

"Remember what the Judge told you, no mum stomp-ing today, be a good coward today."

"Don't step on our property now, be careful."

"Hey Rudy, can you see the cameras. They are watch-ing you right now being a fool."

He never said one word back. Was this childish on my behalf, bet your house? Yes it was. This was not me, yet it was me. It just felt good to respond to him standing there. Something in me kept hoping that I could reach them. I thought that last insult I mentioned would get to him. He never answered me or uttered a word, just that cold stare. This standing on the edge of his property star-ing at us, became the new routine. I would tell myself OK, less than seven, less that, six months now I think we can make it. I pictured him going in to tell Bulla the latest statement. I told myself if he confronted me about my one liners, I would respond with:

"Come on now, some of those had to get a little smile on that rock like scowl you have on your face."

Just when we could not think of anything else they could do it happened. Yes, they came up with still another form of harassment. They would pick a random day and time when we both were home and just stand on the public sidewalk in front of the house and stare into our porch. The dog would go crazy, just doing what dogs do, jumping at the windows, barking, protecting her house. As we looked out, we could see their lips move, but could not make out what they were saying. I had thought to hide a listening device out there and Barbara talked me out of it. She was killing my fun again. They would keep it up until we observed them standing there for a while. I asked Barbara if we could block out the front porch windows and the answer was no. They were not going to control us. I disagreed, but went with the "not shut in" look. I just keep telling myself: "In less than six months all this will be over."

They obviously had memorized the entire city code or at least the index, dam technology. I wondered if they had a computer or they would just call city hall with their ideas. There was a city ordinance about excessive barking. Yes, they started to call the police complaining of excessive barking. One of them would go into call and the other would stand in front of our house until they observed the squad car turn the corner, then the one left outside would retreat to their property line by their house looking into our porch to make sure the dog would keep barking until the police car showed up. The police gave us a warning ticket about the excessive barking. I explained to the police what they were doing to cause the barking and got the old; "it is the law" answer, with some advice to keep the dog off of the front porch. From then on Bou Bou could not go on the front porch. Individually these things may seem minor, yet they have a miserable effect on the place you call home, and they knew it.

HE SLIPPED

It was a Sunday. A love thy neighbour Sunday, I was
on our front porch looking out at the sunny day when
I saw Bulla leaving the house. She headed south
towards the convenience store, did not think she noticed
me on the porch as I was rather slouched down on the
couch out there. Once a month, more or less, she would
venture out of their house to pick up some milk or just to
take a walk on a nice sunny day. The snow was still piled
on either side of the sidewalk, although quite a bit had
melted. The sun that day was melting more of the snow.
The temperatures right around freezing, no wind, and
with the sun out it was quite a nice day for a walk. I was
sitting there about ten minutes when Rudy came out with
his broom to attend to; I don't know what? I observed him
coming down the walk in front of his house stopping on

the clean sidewalk, he must have seen something on the snow covered grass under his front windows. He looked for a good spot to scale the small mound of snow next to the front sidewalk. He found an entry point and began to scale the small mound of snow when, in a flash his feet flew out from under him and he fell backwards in the process hitting his head pretty hard on the sidewalk. He lay there motionless. My coat and gloves were handy so I put them on not knowing how long I would be outside. Going to help him was just something that a person would do to help another in time of crisis. His head was on the cement and his legs from the waist down were still on the snow. When I walked up to him, he was conscious but seemed a bit out of it. He asked me to help him up. I grabbed him by both shoulders and began to help him up. He was heavier than I thought or I was weaker that I thought. After he came to a little, he realized it was me helping him up. He exclaimed "Not you," and jerked away, slipping out of my grasp. His weight, along with him over reacting to get out of my grip, caused him to break free of my grasp with some force, which carried him backwards and his head hit the cement once more. I will never forget that sound. It was like a coconut landing on the sidewalk after being dropped from two stories up. A deep hollow sound, one that I never heard before and will never forget, I just knew it was bad. I looked down beginning to say I'm sorry and saw the blood running down the sidewalk. His eyes where open, I looked at his chest and the coat was not moving. Oh, that sound gave me the chills as it echoed in my mind.

"Rudy, get up, wake up, don't you do this to me. Why did you pull away? I was trying to help you."

He just stared into the sky, not blinking. He lay there motionless, in a strange silence. I was pretty sure his head was already cracked when I first walked up to him, the second blow must have taken him out. I ran to the house to call 911. I made the call and sat on the porch waiting for a ambulance to show up. While waiting for the medics, it became obvious to me that if the second time he struck his head proved to be fatal, I could be accused of murder. I watched enough movies to know about motive and being placed at the scene of the crime in addition to an overzealous prosecuting attorney who was trying to make his mark in the legal profession. All the times they called the police making their outrageous insinuations about us, made this situation really look like I had done something sinister. Everyone in jail says they are innocent, right now I believed half of them.

Did anyone see me out there? If someone did it would certainly appear that I forced him down. Hell, only me, Rudy's ghost and God would know the truth, about what had happened. Thank God Bulla was not home, or she would have been out there swearing I did it. Thinking back I should never have gone outside or called 911, but at the time it was the right thing to do. I did not know if he was dead. I thought so, yet I did not know for sure. I just should of called 911, no time to think at a time like that, you just do what you were taught to do and that was to try and help. When I saw him slip, I thought that possibly I could do something to help him. The paramedics showed up shortly I stayed in the house, not wanting to get near the place of the accident again. The police showed up with the ambulance, just a coincidence that they had arrived at the same time, they came down the street from north and south of the street. Because someone died they yellow taped the area and took many pictures of the taped off area. One of the officers pointed to the camera man to take pictures of the snow, which would show him slipping on the icy snow. The marks in the snow would show his feet slipped out from under him on the snow causing him to fall backwards. The officer, who came over to question me, was an officer I knew from previous complaints from Rudy.

"Did you call 911?"

"Yes Sir"

"He is dead. What did you see?"

I looked down and swallowed hard: "I was on my front porch and noticed he tried to get up the bank into his front yard from the sidewalk,and half way up the snow mound, his feet flew out from under him throwing him backwards."

"Is that all you saw?"

"Yes, it looked like he really hit his head and when I didn't see him move, I called 911."

I sat on the couch looking down, as I was upset, not at him being dead, but for myself probably going to be accused of something I did not do. The fact that he was dead did not bother me. The way it happens on the network shows it seems every time someone, even if they were in law enforcement, was involved in a gory death scene, they got an upset stomach and threw up. I had no such feelings. I guess the fact that I did not do anything to cause his death intentionally made the difference. Forgive me for saying this, to be quite honest I was glad, that sorry excuse for a human being was gone. The officer took me at my word, with no one else to question. He had me sign a statement and bid me a farewell.

I was still on the porch so I put my coat on and went out to see if Bulla was on her way home from the store. When living next to someone, you learn their habits very well. Sometimes she would take a short cut and enter her house through the back door if the neighbour to the rear of Bulla's house driveway was clear of snow. I caught a quick glanced her coming home the back way. I was at a vantage point where she most likely did not see me, so I went back in my house and waited for her reaction when she looked out her front window. She came screaming out of her house.

"My Rudy, where is my Rudy."

A detective pulled her to the side and delivered the unfortunate news. They had removed the body by the time she came running out.

I could hear her screaming through the glass as I watched on the porch.

"It was Thomas," as she pointed to me standing on the front enclosed porch. She was so loud I could hear every word.

"Thomas murdered him. I saw him throw Rudy to the ground and then he called 911. I had come in the back door so Thomas did not see me come home from the store. When I saw him throw Rudy to the ground, the horror of it made me pass out. I fainted when I saw him do that. The next thing I remember is seeing you people out here. Arrest that animal Thomas and throw away the key. I want him to die in prison."

A different detective opened an investigation. He came back to my house. I observed him coming and held open the door for him to come in to talk to me. He made me go over the details of what I had seen. I gave him the exact same story I gave the other officer and signed yet another statement.

"Right now, Thomas it does not look good for you, with her statement."

"Sure, but as usual she is lying. She was at the store when he slipped, you must investigate that."

"He stopped me and asked what store?" I said the closest one just for milk or bread is the gas station con-venience store. She returned in about thirty minutes, so that is my best guess. With that dyed black hair and frequently shopping at that store, the clerk should remember her and if she used a credit card the time would be on there. Those places usually have camera's, don't they?"

"Thomas, let us do the police work."

"I understand but you must know, she was not home when the accident happened."

"For your sake, I hope we can find proof of that. She is going to sign a formal statement that she indeed saw you kill him. Do not leave town."

I began to perspire. I sat on the couch afraid that I was going to faint. When I recovered somewhat I called a friend who was a criminal attorney. I explained what had happen and wondered what was next. He explained as follows:

"If there is a formal charge the availability of bail would depend upon the specific charge. There are several charges that can result from a death – murder (intention), manslaughter (sudden rage, reckless disregard, firearm involved) or involuntary manslaughter (criminal negligence.) If you where to be arrested it would very hard to get bail on an intentional murder charge. Assuming bail is available in your state the bail could be millions of dollars. It would be easier if it were a manslaughter case, but still expensive. The best case scenario would be involuntary manslaughter, and depending on the circumstances, bail might be two hundred thousand dollars.

If the court sets bail at $1 million, the defendant would have to provide cash or other assets equal to $100,000. For a lesser crime, a bail of $200,000 would only require a $20,000 bond in Illinois. Also an acquittal in a criminal case could still leave you vulnerable to a civil suit for wrongful death."

To say the least, I was frightened beyond belief. I guessed the next step would be just waiting for the door bell to ring with the news from the police. I could not go to work I just sat on the couch waiting for a decision that could affect the rest of my life. Three of the longest days of my life crawled by with little sleep. On the third day at 4:00 p.m. a detectives car pulled up and parked in-between our houses on the street, blocking me from backing out of my driveway. He got out of his car and began walking to my house. The air went out of me. I think I just stopped breathing, but realizing this, I forced myself to take slow breaths so I would not pass out. I let him in by holding the door open. He entered looking me straight in the eyes.

"Thomas, she used her credit card which put the time of your 911 call and her presence being at the convenience store at the same time. She claimed to be passed out in her house, when she was actually at the store. Now if you will excuse me I must arrest someone for filing a false police report of murder."

I wanted to talk to him, and he knew it, but he would not discuss anything further with me about her arrest. I started to ask him a question and he told me to talk to my attorney. I had not realized it, but for those three days my shoulders were as tight as a wound up rope, when he left I could feel them unwind.

I called my attorney friend who taught law for pre-law college students. He cited (720 ILCS 5/26-1) (4) "Transmits or causes to be transmit in any manner to any peace officer, public employee a report to effect that an offense will be committed, is being committed, or has been committed, knowing at the time of such transmission that there is no reasonable ground for believing that such an offense will be committed, is being committed, or has been committed." In Illinois perjury is a Class 3 felony offense punishable by 2-5 years in prison not to mention a large fine.

When Rudy was alive he made sure they did not sign a police report. They always called the police but would never sign a statement or complaint. He should have explained to her in greater detail the reason for his refusal ever to sign. With him not here to stop her from putting her signature on a statement witnessing a murder, the deed was done. She signed the statement and sealed her fate. Could there be something to the belief in humanity that embraces the theory of good and bad Karma?

www.ingramcontent.com/pod-product-compliance
Lightning Source LLC
Chambersburg PA
CBHW060847280326
41934CB00007B/956